OUR
NEW
ZEALAND

OUR
NEW
ZEALAND

a celebration of our
NATIONAL TREASURES
& PLEASURES

RANDOM HOUSE
NEW ZEALAND

Contents

Introduction

It's a big ask to sum up what makes a nation tick, and what its people treasure and love. It can be done by selecting objects, music, poems, songs, recipes, heroes and touchstones that stand for the myriad strands which combine to create a national culture.

That's what this book seeks to do — it's a sampler of our storehouse of treasures, for you to take home to be part of yours.

WHO ARE WE?

N ew Zealand, Enzed, Aotearoa, the
Antipodes, Godzone, Down Under . . . It's
a little country at the bottom of the world,
on exactly the other side of the globe from
Europe. Three main islands and many small
ones, with an estimated 15,000 kilometres
of coastline, set amid the roaring forties of
the Southern Ocean, 1500 kilometres from
the nearest major land mass, it is indeed as
Rudyard Kipling described: 'Last, loneliest,
loveliest, exquisite, apart . . .'

New Zealand was settled by Pacific people around the thirteenth century. It was first visited by European explorers and exploiters in the 1600s, then in increasing numbers from the late 1700s. Following annexation by the British Empire in 1840, European, mainly British, settlers came in their hundreds, then thousands, felling the native forests to create farms, building towns, and clashing with the original inhabitants of the land in a series of wars from the 1860s.

In 1907 New Zealand became a dominion in its own right, but remained tied to Mother England's apron strings; on the outbreak of war in 1939, Prime Minister Michael Joseph Savage declared 'where [Britain] goes, we go'. But a national identity separate from that of 'Home' was emerging, as cohorts of second-, third- and fourth-generation New Zealanders began to grow up and take note of the things which made this country different from any other.

Mid-twentieth-century New Zealand was often considered by its younger inhabitants to be conservative, narrow-minded and isolated: pubs shut at six o'clock, shops were closed at weekends and import duties placed heavy restrictions on the availability of consumer goods. The economic reforms of the 1980s changed all that, dragging New Zealand — with some kicking and screaming — into the modern world.

International air travel and, more recently, internet communication have brought us closer to the rest of the world. As well as natural growth, immigration has produced a lively, multicultural society which would be all but unrecognisable to the pioneers of 150 years earlier.

Today we are a diverse bunch, tracing our origins from a wide range of countries and cultures. New Zealand remains a nation of immigrant origins, but with strong roots now planted in a local soil. Being here, growing strong under the South Pacific sky, has produced a distinctive cultural identity which is more than a sum of its parts.

This, then, is a collection of the things New Zealanders love, the places, people and pastimes we hold sacred. Many of them are simple pleasures — we're not a sophisticated bunch. This is our land and these are our songs, our stories, our experiences. This is Our New Zealand.

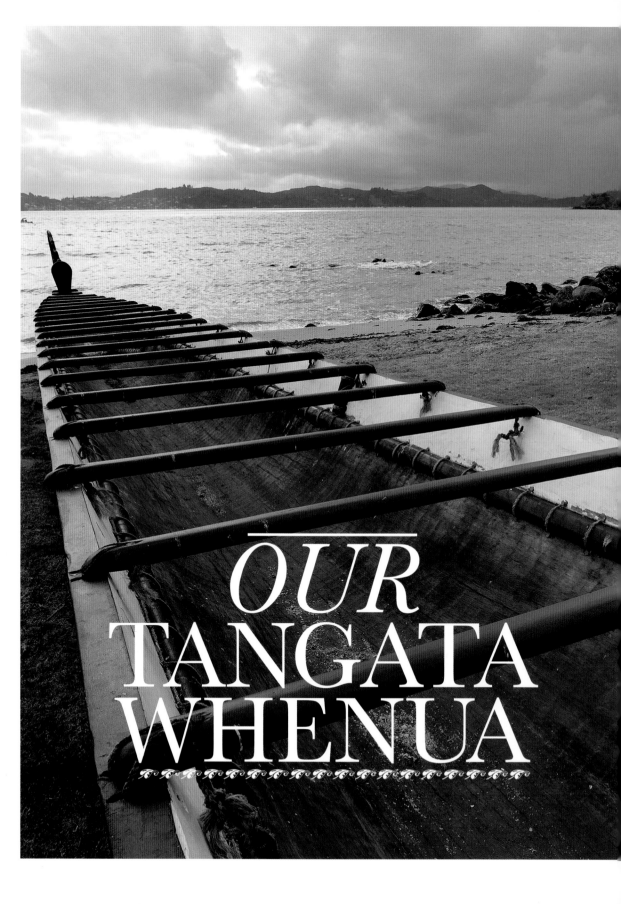

OUR
TANGATA
WHENUA

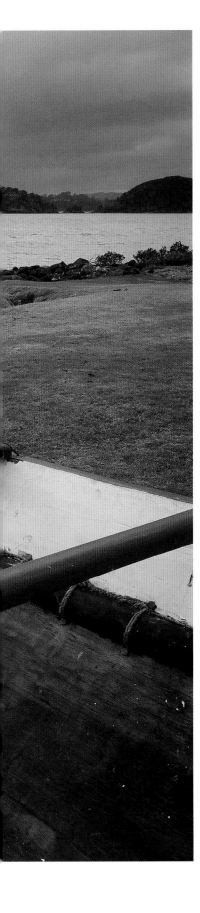

M

āori are tangata whenua — people of the land — and they have a special relationship with the country they call Aotearoa, the land of the long white cloud.

At the 2006 census, out of just over four million New Zealanders, a little more than 500,000 people identified as Māori. (This is the most recent census with published results; the 2011 event was postponed for two years because of the Canterbury earthquakes.)

Te reo Māori, the Māori language, and Māori customs are part of everyday life for most New Zealanders, of all ethnic backgrounds.

Around the thirteenth century, Māori arrived from eastern Polynesia, having made journeys that are widely regarded as epic feats of navigation and endurance. The descendants of those who arrived in the great canoes *Aotea*, *Kurahaupō*, *Mataatua*, *Tainui*, *Tokomaru*, *Te Arawa* and *Tākitimu*, and many others, formed distinct tribal groupings throughout the two main islands. Early Māori were hunter-gatherers and had a rich birdlife available as a protein source; but they were also agriculturalists, which allowed the population to expand. When the first European explorers and, later, sealers, whalers and traders showed up, from the late eighteenth century on, they found plenty of prosperous Māori settlements, both along the coast and inland.

By the turn of the nineteenth century, both inter-tribal wars (which were deadly affairs once Māori had acquired muskets) and European

diseases had taken their toll on the Māori population. Alienation from their tribal lands under the pressure of newly arriving and land-hungry immigrant settlers, and bitter wars in some districts during the 1860s against British troops, were further, almost fatal, blows.

For several decades Māori were considered a dying race, and use of the language was discouraged. In the first half of the twentieth century, however, leaders such as Sir Apirana Ngata spearheaded a revival of Māori culture and language. This movement was echoed in the 1970s, a period known as the Māori Renaissance. The Waitangi Tribunal was established in 1975 to investigate breaches of the 1840 treaty between Māori and the British Crown, and te reo Māori became recognised as an official language of New Zealand by Act of Parliament in 1987.

TE REO MĀORI

Te reo Māori is in frequent usage in official documents and by government departments, at events and in schools. The 2006 census showed that around a quarter of Māori aged 15 to 64 years could hold a conversation in te reo Māori, and most New Zealanders know at least a handful of common words likely to be encountered in everyday life, from the cheery 'kia ora' (gidday), to sitting down for a hui (meeting) or a kōrero (chat), giving a koha (gift), or having some kai (food) or a hangi (meal cooked in an earth oven).

MĀORI WORDS IN COMMON USAGE

SALUTATIONS

kia ora	hi (general informal greeting)
haere mai	welcome, come
tēnā koe	formal greeting to one person
tēnā koutou	formal greeting to many people
ka kite anō/ ka kite	see you soon (informal goodbye)
haere rā	goodbye (from a person staying)
e noho rā	goodbye (from a person leaving)
hei konā rā	goodbye (less formal)

THE MARAE

hui	a meeting of any kind, conference, gathering
marae	the area in front of a meeting house or applied to a whole marae complex
tangata whenua	original people belonging to a place, local people, hosts
tangihanga/ tangi	funeral ceremony
haka	chant with dance for the purpose of challenge
waiata	song or chant which follows a speech

koha	gift, present (usually money, can be food or precious items, given by guest to hosts)

CONCEPTS

aroha	compassion, tenderness, sustaining love
mana	authority, power; reputation, influence
manaakitanga	respect for hosts or kindness to guests; to entertain, to look after
mauri	hidden essential life force or a symbol of this
taihoa	to delay, to wait, to hold off to allow maturation of plans, etc.
taonga	treasured possessions or cultural items, anything precious
tapu	sacred, not to be touched, to be avoided because sacred
tino rangatiratanga	the highest possible independent chiefly authority, paramount authority, sometimes used for 'sovereignty'
tūrangawaewae	a place to stand, a place to belong to, a seat or location of identity

whakapapa	genealogy, to recite genealogy, to establish kin connections	
whenua	land, homeland, country; also afterbirth, placenta	

PEOPLE AND THEIR GROUPS

hapū	sub-tribe
iwi	tribe
waka	canoe, canoe group (all the iwi and hapū descended from the crew of a founding waka)
whānau	extended or non-nuclear family
whanaunga	kin, relatives
Pākehā	the Māori word for people living in New Zealand of British/European origin
kaumātua	elder or elders
kuia	elderly lady
koro	elderly man
rangatira	person of chiefly rank, boss, owner
tipuna/tupuna	ancestor
tama	son, young man, youth
tamāhine	daughter
tamariki	children
tāne	man, husband, men, husbands
wahine	woman, wife (wāhine = women, wives)

COMPONENTS OF PLACE NAMES

iti	little, e.g. Rotoiti
kai	one meaning is food; in a place name it signifies a place where a particular food source was plentiful, e.g. Kaikōura
maunga	mountain, e.g. Maunganui
moana	sea or large lake, e.g. Taupō Moana
motu	island, e.g. Motutapu
nui	big, e.g. Maunganui
puke	hill, e.g. Pukekohe
roto	lake, e.g. Rotorua
wai	water, e.g. Waitemata
whanga	harbour, bay, e.g. Whangarei

THE MĀORI CREATION MYTH

How was the world created? Out of the darkness came Rangi and Papa, sky father and earth mother. They have many sons, who are locked forever between earth and sky in their parents' embrace, but they yearn to see the light. Here is how author and poet Robert Sullivan tells the story.

It began before anything — before the beginning, before there was night to set apart from daylight, before there were the insects that fill our heads with their sounds as we sleep.

Zzz.

There wasn't anything! If you'd been there you would have seen nothing, for colour didn't exist, air wasn't there; the very idea of space couldn't have been there because there were no ideas at all. There was absolutely nothing. And I mean nothing in the entire universe. No planets. No stars. No sun or moon. Nothing we could touch and call home.

In this place before time, there was emptiness. This went on for a long time — or maybe just for a twinkling instant of the blink of an eye, the flashing of an eyelid, because there was no time to measure this by, back then.

Not an atom stirred. Everything was hushed. Waiting. The very nothingness before the massive universe of today seemed to be crouched and waiting. Waiting for a shadow to fall. Waiting for the spirit that makes everything alive to arrive.

But something must have changed because the old people started talking about 'the night'.

A sense of night came upon the universe. Here was something: it was night. Night after night. Many nights. Uncountable nights. Long and deep nights. Nights without daylight to break them. Nights without twilight to start them. These were the nights just grazing the birth

of the universe, before the births of the gods, and before the births of their descendants, the people of Aotearoa New Zealand.

The births of the gods is a mystery. Some things are meant to be mysterious — just like the births of constellations of stars are a mystery for scientists today. Just like the creation of the entire universe is a mystery. But scientists don't use that word — 'mystery'.

Out of the mystery came Ranginui, the sky father, and Papatūānuku, the earth mother. Just like parents who live together today, Rangi and Papa loved each other very much. They loved each other in the beginning of time. Their love was so complete they were completely satisfied. They didn't need the things we need today — they were so complete with each other. They were in a huge embrace, a great big hug. They were gods, remember. They were massive massive gods — as massive as the planet, as massive as the sky.

Rangi and Papa's huge embrace left the world we know in darkness. Not a peep of light shone through between them. If you were an insect you couldn't wriggle into a space that let the light through. The world was a dark place. But it must have been a loving place, too. Imagine such enormous love between the sky and earth!

Like all parents, they had children. (Well, they couldn't be parents without children, could they?) Some people say they had seventy children. Like themselves, the children of Ranginui and Papatūānuku were gods. Tall gods, skinny gods, wide gods: gods that lived in the folds of the earth mother, and gods that lived slightly higher up with the sky father. Imagine a world so close that you could reach the sky by standing upright. You'd hit your head on the heavens! Such was the closeness of the earth and the sky, the mother and the father.

The young gods were growing, and unfortunately for their parents, they were growing angry, frustrated at being squished so closely between their parents. They were tired of walking around on all fours. Tired of the sky father's armpits, tired of being ignored by their parents, who only had time to hug each other it seemed. Imagine seventy angry young men! For they were all boy gods.

Oh, there was one who wasn't angry — Tāwhirimātea, the God of Winds. He was happy with the ways of the world he lived in. The closeness of his parents. It must have felt wonderful to feel the radiant energy of his father so close to the earthiness of his mother. Being a god of the air, I suppose the lack of space didn't worry him in the least. He liked playing with his parents. He'd blow on the vines tying the earth to the sky, so they chuckled and twanged in the quiet scrub. There weren't any forests yet because there wasn't enough room. Just enough for little bushes, and creeping plants. No wonder the other brothers were so grumpy!

The brothers had a meeting. It was tricky. They had to crouch down so there would be enough space for them all. They were planning something very secretly so their parents wouldn't overhear them. That was tricky since Ranginui was right overhead and might easily hear the scheming brothers' plans. They mumbled and muttered, laughed and grumbled. They argued about who was going to do this secret thing. Who was going to help?

Tāwhirimātea was angry and refused to help. He felt threatened.

Quickly then, the other brothers began their secret plan. First to try was Rongomatane, the God of all the good food that people tend and nurture for their bellies. He tried his hardest; he gave it his best, most god-like effort. He tried and tried and tried with all his might, but still he could not do the secret thing. (Luckily, his parents had no idea what he was up to.)

Then Tangaroa gave a god-like crack with one of his tidal waves, for he was the God of the Oceans. He gurgled. He spluttered. He blew bubbles. But even the God of the Oceans couldn't make the secret plan work. And Ranginui and Papatūānuku still didn't know. The parents just kept on hugging.

Then Haumia-tikitiki, the God of all the food that we find growing in the wild, put his mind to the secret task. He tried so hard that he needed a sit-down afterwards. But even he failed. It seemed this thing would never happen. The brothers would be sitting in the darkness forever and a day.

(Oops, I almost let the secret out of the bag.) Well, the next god said he wasn't going to sit around all day. He was a fuming sort of god. He was really angry. He looked really mean. But remember, even if the gods sound mean, they are just doing their job. For this was Tūmatauenga, the God of War. Tūmatauenga was going to fight the powers. He was going to fight with all his angry, shouting might.

He applied every little thought in his head to carrying out the secret plan. He focused so hard he couldn't think of anything else in the whole wide and low world. But he failed. He couldn't do it and it made him

mad! (But being mad is one of his jobs, remember. He is the God of War after all.)

Tūmatauenga looked over at his brother Tāne Mahuta. 'What are you doing?' he roared, even though it was a question. (Most people when they ask a question make their voices go upwards a bit, so they sound polite, but not Tūmatauenga.) Tāne ignored his younger brother. He just lay there.

Then Tāne made the plan work!

'What plan?' you might ask.

The plan all the gods, except Tāwhirimātea, had made in secret and been trying to carry out for ages.

He lay on his back, and placed his feet very carefully on his father's body. He didn't want to hurt him. He loved his parents. He just wanted more space. More light and air. Light for all the plants and birds and insects of Tāne, for he was God of the Forest and father of many creatures.

Very slowly, quite gently but firmly too, he pushed his feet up a bit. Some of the vines holding the sky and the earth together began to spring, and rustle, even snap. He pushed again. Twang! Every vine between the huge parents snapped. Again he pushed and with every push the father rose a bit further. Tāne kept pushing. Higher and higher his father went. He used his hands to press down into the soil of his mother. She went lower as Ranginui went higher. High above the beloved earth mother, Papatūānuku. Soon Ranginui, the sky father, the great parent, the greatest husband of the greatest wife, was out of reach. Tāne, the lord of the forest, had separated his parents forever.

That was the secret. The great beginning of the world we know. The separation of the sky and the earth. The first time light shone upon the earth.

Even the most unemotional New Zealanders feel a lump in their throats when the New Zealand flag is raised at events such as the Olympic Games. Don't confuse it with the Australian flag — ours has four stars, not six, and they're red with white borders. And the Union flag in the corner is a constant reminder of our origins as a little piece of England half a world away.

OUR
FLAG

For its first 60 or so years as a British colony, New Zealand didn't have a flag. Ships registered in the colony flew the British blue ensign — essentially the same flag without the stars — from the 1860s; the four points of the Southern Cross were added in 1869. The flag became officially recognised in 1902 and is flown from government buildings and high-profile places such as the Auckland Harbour Bridge (except in strong wind conditions) every day.

The government also officially recognises the Māori national or Tino Rangatiratanga flag. Designed by a collective of Māori women artists, the flag was first flown, alongside the New Zealand flag, on Waitangi Day in 1990, on the 150th anniversary of the signing of the treaty. This flag is now frequently flown on marae and around the country on Waitangi Day. Also often flown at Waitangi and around the north is the flag of the United Tribes, designed by missionary Henry Williams and flown unofficially as New Zealand's flag and on New Zealand-built ships prior to the signing of the treaty in 1840.

OUR STARS

The first visitors to the southern hemisphere navigated by the stars, and were astounded by what they found. Many familiar constellations appeared upside down to those from the north, and a striking cross was visible in the night sky, seen by the navigators as a sign from God. This is the Southern Cross, which moves around the sky and even turns upside down — but always points the way south. It has become a national icon, the stars of our flag.

Orion, another easily recognisable constellation, appears inverted in our night sky — instead of a giant's sparkly belt, we see a pot we call 'the Big Dipper'. In the far south, the Aurora Australis or Southern Lights can be seen playing in the sky on long summer evenings.

Early Māori also used the stars for navigation, and to keep track of the seasons. The first appearance of Matariki (the constellation known as the Pleiades or the Seven Sisters in the classical world) in late May or early June marks the start of the Māori New Year.

Visitors to New Zealand are often stunned by the profusion of stars visible in our night sky, especially away from the light pollution of the major cities. The Milky Way appears as a bright smear across the sky, and meteors are frequently seen. In 2012, Lake Tekapo in southern Canterbury became officially recognised as one of the best places in the world to stargaze, with a 4300 square kilometre 'dark sky' reserve officially recognised by the International Dark-Sky Association.

OUR SHAKY ISLES

New Zealanders are used to the earth moving beneath their feet. The first European settlers in New Zealand found out pretty quickly that it was an unstable place. In 1855, when the settlement of Wellington was just 15 years old, the largest earthquake yet recorded in New Zealand struck the nearby Wairarapa region. In Wellington itself, a large area of seabed was raised up to form dry land, creating the land on which much of today's central business district stands. As the city had a small population at the time, only a handful of people were killed.

The same could not be said of the Hawke's Bay in 1931, when 256 people were killed in a magnitude 7.8 earthquake which virtually destroyed the city of Napier. It was later rebuilt in the Art Deco style which now underpins its identity.

Memories fade. New Zealanders had perhaps become rather blasé about the possibility of a major shake occurring until, out of the blue, a magnitude 7.1 earthquake hit Canterbury on Saturday, 4 September 2010, causing widespread property damage but no loss of life. New Zealanders heaved a collective sigh of relief, but the region — and the country as a whole — took a body-blow on Tuesday, 22 February 2011, when a smaller but more shallow quake hit much closer to the centre of the city of Christchurch. Central-city streets and buildings were full of people going about their daily business; 185 people were killed and thousands injured, and it will take years for the city's central business district and infrastructure to be restored.

Still, there are upsides to living in a country strung out along a faultline. Despite the frequency of small to moderate earthquakes, and the occasional big one, we are blessed with the volcanic wonders of the Rotorua region and the Central Plateau, and there are many places where natural hot water bubbles up freely out of the ground. We have learned to take the rough with the smooth.

W e have two national anthems, one being 'God Save the Queen'. 'God Defend New Zealand' is the song most often wheeled out at rugby games and on state occasions. The stentorian Victorian words come from a poem written by Irish immigrant journalist Thomas Bracken, and were set to music as part of a competition in 1876 — Otago schoolteacher John Joseph Woods apparently dashed off the music in a single sitting.

It became our national song in 1940, in time for the celebrations of the centennial of the Treaty of Waitangi, and a joint national anthem (with the permission of Queen Elizabeth II) in 1977. A Māori version of 'God Defend New Zealand' was first written in 1878, and this version is now sung as often as the English (often before it).

OUR NATIONAL ANTHEM

Māori version
E Ihowā Atua
O ngā iwi mātou rā
Āta whakarangona
Me aroha noa
Kia hua ko te pai
Kia tau tō atawhai
Manaakitia mai

English version
God of Nations at Thy feet
In the bonds of love we meet
Hear our voices, we entreat
God defend our free land
Guard Pacific's triple star
From the shafts of strife and war
Make her praises heard afar

OUR
MOST FAMOUS
HAKA

It sends a chill up the spine of the toughest sporting opponent, not to mention the crowd: a semicircle of men in black, slapping their thighs, rolling their eyes and chanting the words of a challenge, a haka. It's impressive when any bunch of Kiwis breaks into the haka, whether it is the All Blacks or a bunch of uncoordinated Pākehā celebrating on foreign soil.

The haka or Māori war dance most often performed by the All Blacks (and many other New Zealand sporting teams) is 'Ka Mate', composed by warrior chief Te Rauparaha in the 1810s and describing how he escaped from enemies by hiding in a food storage pit. Performing the 'war cry' before the start of a game has been a tradition since the earliest days of All Black rugby.

Ka mate, ka mate!
I die, I die
Ka ora, ka ora!
I live, I live
Ka mate, ka mate!
I die, I die
Ka ora! ka ora!
I live, I live

Tēnei te tangata pūhuruhuru
Nāna nei i tiki mai whakawhiti te rā
Ā, upane! Ka upane!
Ā, upane, ka upane, whiti te rā!
Hī!

This is the hairy man
Who caused the sun to shine again for me
Up the ladder, up the ladder
Up to the top
The sun shines!
Rise!

OUR SPLENDID WILD PLACES

New Zealand is a country of just four and a half million inhabitants spread out over around 270,000 square kilometres of land, the vast majority of people living in a handful of cities around its coastline. Despite the encroachment of settlements and farming, vast tracts of countryside are untouched bush or mountain, all but devoid of people. Here are some of our favourite wild places.

THE
MANIOTOTO

The Maniototo Plain lies between coastal Otago and 'Central', the mountainous hinterland of the South Island province famous for its skifields and wineries. Exploited by gold miners in the 1860s, the Maniototo is now splendidly empty — home to hardy farmers, artists such as Grahame Sydney, poets such as Brian Turner, and a growing tourist industry based around the abandoned Central Otago railway line, now a popular route for cyclists.

FIORDLAND NATIONAL PARK

The World Heritage area of Fiordland spreads from the deep and cold southern lakes of Te Anau and Manapouri to the even deeper and colder fiords of Milford and Doubtful Sounds. Much of the area is preserved as a national park. Its topography makes it largely inaccessible, giving rise to rumours of the persistence of species such as the extinct moa, the elusive and extremely rare kākāpō and even the introduced moose. The park includes some of New Zealand's great walks: the Milford, Routeburn and Kepler tracks — which some ultrasport enthusiasts take on as a one-day, 60-kilometre mountain run.

NINETY MILE BEACH

This lonely strip of surf-beaten sand — not 90 miles long in fact, but more like 60, or 96 kilometres — stretches towards the northern tip of New Zealand, along the wild west coast. Its Māori name is Te Oneroa a Tōhē (the long beach of Tōhē), after the journey made by an ancestor of the Muriwhenua tribes. It is considered sacred, being the pathway of the spirits of the dead as they travel to Cape Reinga, where they leap into the sea for the final leg of their journey to the mythical homeland of Hawaiki. The beach is still legally a road, and is traversed daily by tourist buses making the loop to the Cape. At other times, it's the vast fishing ground of surfcasters on the lookout for big snapper.

TONGARIRO
NATIONAL
PARK

New Zealand's first national park — and the fourth in the world — was gifted to the nation by Te Heuheu Tukino, a chief of the Ngāti Tūwharetoa tribe, in 1887. The park encompasses the peaks of Tongariro, Ngauruhoe and Ruapehu, the last hosting the only commercial skifields in the North Island. The volcanoes are still restless: Ruapehu erupted in 1995 and again in 1996, and Tongariro gave an unexpected sneeze of ash and rocks in mid-2012 for the first time in 100 years — another sign that these are shaky isles indeed.

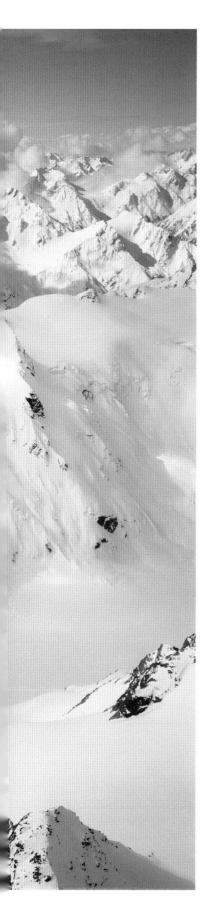

THE SOUTHERN ALPS

The Southern Alps, lying along the Alpine Fault, are the icy spine of the South Island. These mountains have been pushed up and ground down to sea level many times over millions of years, although the peaks we see today are young in geographical terms, at a mere five million years old. Their highest point — and the summit of New Zealand — is Aoraki Mt Cook, at 3754 metres, but it is surrounded by 19 other peaks which are more than 3000 metres above sea level. The Alps form the backdrop to South Island life — their tips permanently covered in snow, while at their feet braided rivers flow across rich alluvial plains.

OUR FARMS

Those who fly across New Zealand for the first time could be forgiven for thinking it was one big farm. In the main, our small cities and towns are scattered across a green and rolling landscape where livestock considerably outnumber people.

Early Māori were small-scale horticulturalists, tending plots of kūmara, a variety of sweet potato. The waves of European settlers who arrived from the 1840s onwards found a fertile new country with a temperate climate, where even the most lowly of agricultural labourers could buy his own plot, breaking it in from virgin forest and making a living from the rich soil beneath.

New Zealand may no longer be a predominantly rural country by population, but our pastoral roots run deep and our love of the land remains.

We owe a lot to the sheep. We still have just over 30 million of them, around seven sheep for every person — down from a peak of 70 million in the early 1980s — and this country is still the world's largest exporter of sheep meat and wool.

Sheep are tough, and breeds like merino do well on our steep, dry hillsides and in alpine pastures, where the runholders on sprawling sheep stations still bring them down from the high country (or 'tops'), mustering in the traditional way with dogs and horses. We've bred our own varieties too, such as the Corriedale, Perendale and Drysdale.

There isn't any way to get the wool off a sheep's back each year except by hand and, unsurprisingly, New Zealand has produced some of the world's best shearers. Shearers were traditionally paid by the number of sheep shorn, so speed and efficiency were prized from the earliest days.

The pursuit is professional now; each year a national competition, the Golden Shears, is held in Masterton in the Wairarapa region, and New Zealand shearers have made their name on the world shearing stage too. Top performers can shear more than 700 sheep in a nine-hour day — you'd deserve a beer after that.

For many New Zealanders, each day begins before sunrise. In the pre-dawn quiet, Friesian and Jersey cows slowly move their way down well-worn tracks to the bright lights of the milking shed, where 12 hours' worth of milky goodness will be pumped from their udders and trucked away to the dairy factory.

The same process is repeated in the afternoons, every day of the year, weekdays and weekends, summer and winter (although the cows get some time off to calve each year). This is the cycle of the dairy farmer's life.

Dairying is New Zealand's largest export industry, with 95 per cent of our milk, cream, butter, cheese and associated products heading overseas. Most of this business is controlled by Fonterra, a giant farmers' collective responsible for about one-third of the world's dairy trade.

We keep our cows outside, in paddocks, and let them eat grass. The idea of factory farming and feedlots makes our collective toes curl. Around 80 per cent of our output of Angus, Hereford and shorthorn beef is sent overseas, but there's still plenty left over to slap on the barbecue.

And then there are our arable farmers, growing wheat, oats, rye and barley; our orchardists; our tobacco growers; our horticulturalists. All are blessed by our fertile soils and temperate climate.

A&P SHOWS

Axemen and candy floss, champion cow parades and sand saucers, show jumping and Highland dancing — the tradition of the annual Agricultural and Pastoral Association (or A&P) show has persisted for more than 100 years, despite New Zealand's increasing urbanisation. It's a day when the country comes to town and, increasingly, town comes to the country, as city-dwellers take a day out to kick tractor tyres and admire alpacas.

The first shows in New Zealand were held in the 1840s, as soon as European farmers had settled in, and today the Royal Agricultural Society still acts as an umbrella organisation for nearly 100 A&P societies throughout the country. The uber-expression of the 'country day out' is the massive National Agricultural Fieldays at Mystery Creek, Hamilton, which attract more than 100,000 people annually.

N

ew Zealand has been a rich subject for painters since the earliest days of European exploration. Some of the first scenes of the country were created by artists who travelled with Captain James Cook on his two visits in 1769–70 and 1773.

THE LAND AND ITS PAINTERS

RITA
ANGUS

/1908–70

Cass
1936
oil on canvas

Rita Angus's image of a country railway station dwarfed by towering hills, with a tiny settlement and rugby goal posts just visible beyond, and where a lonely figure sits, dressed in overcoat and hat, was voted New Zealand's greatest painting in a television poll in 2006. Cass is a speck on the map, a brief stop for a train as it pulls away from the big hill country of the rugged upper Waimakariri Valley and heads for Arthur's Pass and the tunnel buried under the spine of the Southern Alps that will take it to the West Coast.

In the 1930s and 1940s Angus was among the most prominent of a group of regionalist painters who were mostly based in Canterbury and were known as The Group, who sought a modern style of painting that would express New Zealand culture.

WILLIAM
SUTTON
/1917–2000

Nor'wester in the cemetery
1950
oil on canvas

Canterbury painter William Sutton taught at the School of Fine Arts at the University of Canterbury for 40 years. A member of The Group, his *Nor'wester in the cemetery* is vivid and palpable to anyone who has ever been in Canterbury on a scorching day when the nor'west wind roars down from the Southern Alps.

CHRISTOPHER PERKINS

/1891–1968

Taranaki
1931
oil on canvas

British painter Christopher Perkins, who taught art in New Zealand from 1929 to 1934 and who became a champion of a nationalist approach that would develop a local tradition of art, observed that 'the future of New Zealand as a country of painters is guaranteed by its marvellous light' — a statement that's been quoted many times since. Art writer Hamish Keith brilliantly describes Perkins's famous painting: 'The prescription all came together wonderfully in *Taranaki*. There is the crisp, clear style, and the sense of geometric structure that underpins the landscape and its buildings. There is a clarity of light, so hard that it turns the clouds into solid masses and renders the distance as clearly focused as the foreground. There is the narrative detail, the specifically local features of the work . . . the tin shed architecture that forms a central part of Perkins' impressions of New Zealand.'

COLIN
MCCAHON

/1919–87

Northland Panels
1958
oil on canvas

Colin McCahon is one of the heavyweights of New Zealand painting: his style is unmistakable, frequently combining words — often Biblical texts — with bold images. McCahon studied art and began painting in the 1930s, but it wasn't until the late 1950s and 1960s that he began to produce the larger-scale, iconic works for which he is best known. Among the first of these was the *Northland Panels*, initially painted in a single afternoon using house paint on large panels of unstretched canvas. Here McCahon captures 'snapshots' of the Northland landscape: dripping bush, green hills and exposed red clay.

DON BINNEY

/1940–2012

**Sun shall not burn Thee
by day nor moon by night**
1966
oil and acrylic on canvas

Don Binney mostly painted the Northland and Auckland regions, especially Auckland's west coast, where he had spent considerable time as a boy and young man. An early interest in birdwatching explains the strong avian element of his figurative paintings, which frequently also have an environmental theme. Binney taught for many years at the Elam School of Fine Arts in Auckland. He painted this work in 1966; the bird is the rare, flightless mātātā or fernbird, which inhabits protected wetlands.

GRAHAME SYDNEY

/1948–

Timeless Land
1992
oil on linen

Since he began to paint, in the 1970s, Grahame Sydney has turned again and again to documenting the muscular, ancient Hawkdun Range and nearby Mt Saint Bathans rising from a sere plain, through still, serene, finely wrought paintings. It's as if Sydney can't help but look at this empty place over and over again, staring deeper and deeper into its soul — and neither can we.

DICK
FRIZZELL
/1943–

Tarawera Rest Stop
1989
oil on canvas

Dick Frizzell has painted many things in his long and varied career as an artist — cans of tuna, tiki, cartoon characters, boats and roadside signs among them. In the late 1980s he spent four years actively working on landscapes, the period during which this view of a petrol station on the winding and lonely road that separates Taupō from the Hawke's Bay was painted. Primitive in style, and with echoes of Christopher Perkins's earlier work in the same area, it's a road painting that speaks to any motorist who feels the massing of the hills and the towering of the trees when driving through big hill country.

STANLEY
PALMER

/1936–

Cape Maria van Diemen — Waitapu
2002
oil on linen

Stanley Palmer is one of New Zealand's most active contemporary landscape painters, his fine oils on linen capturing our land bathed in a glorious light that makes it appear soft, inviting, caressing, yet also empty and expectant. Cape Maria van Diemen is the westernmost point of the North Island, named by the seventeenth-century Dutch explorer Abel Tasman in honour of the wife of his expedition's sponsor. Palmer shows the view of the cape from the cliffs west of Cape Reinga. Motuopao Island stands just offshore.

BIRDS
WE
LOVE

A country of small islands adrift in the vast Pacific Ocean for millions of years, New Zealand has only two native land mammals, both of which are species of bat. The ecological niches filled elsewhere by animals are here populated by birds, giving a diversity of strange and wonderful species which have evolved into sometimes peculiar forms.

KIWI
Apteryx australis

As you lie in your tent, out of the darkness of the
New Zealand bush comes the call of the kiwi as it
goes about its nightly business. First one whistle,
then another. One bird calls, then its mate, then
one from over there — a rising warble ending in a
shriek. Seldom seen, but increasingly heard as forest
remnants and even more settled areas are rid of pests
and made kiwi-friendly, the kiwi is New Zealand's
national bird. New Zealanders gained the nickname
'Kiwis' as far back as the First World War.

Due to their scarcity and nocturnal habits you'd
be lucky to see one outside of a zoo, but it is a bird
dear to New Zealanders' hearts. Jokes have been
made over the years about how our emblematic
bird lives in the dark, eats worms and can't fly, but
— like rugby hero Dan Carter — boy, can the kiwi
kick! It is also the only bird to have its nostrils at
the tip of its beak, all the better to sniff out tasty
worms and grubs in forest leaf-litter.

KEA
Nestor notabilis

Bouncing down an alpine rock fall, head turned to one side with an air of enquiry, the curious kea approaches as if it wants to be friends. Turn your back, however, and it'll nick the laces out of your boots and steal the rubber off your windscreen wipers. Kea may be known as the vandals of the bird world, but that's only an expression of their high levels of intelligence.

Kea were once common in the high country of the South Island, but were culled in the 1960s and 1970s after a few rogue birds gave the species an undeserved reputation for attacking sheep. Now they are fully protected, and continue to delight visitors to high-country parks such as Arthur's Pass and Aoraki Mt Cook with their laughing 'ke-a' call, inching closer then scooting away with a flash of red from under their wings.

TŪĪ

Prosthemadera novaeseelandiae

Early European visitors to the untouched New Zealand bush were roused by a primal dawn chorus of exquisite beauty; naturalist Joseph Banks, who travelled with Captain James Cook, described it as 'the most melodious wild musick I have ever heard, almost imitating small bells but with the most tuneable silver sound imaginable'.

Even if it is before the sun has come up, there is still something magical about being woken by a tūī, its mellifluous call like that of no other songbird. As well as trills and bell-like notes, its repertoire includes clicks, squeaks, gurgles and super-sonic sections audible only to dogs and children. Clever mimics, tūī have been known to whistle advertising jingles and replicate phone ringtones with confusing accuracy. The tuft of white feathers bobbing at its throat originally earned the bird the name parsonbird.

KĀKĀPŌ
Strigops habroptilus

In a land of strange and wonderful birds, the kākāpō is one of the strangest. It is the world's largest parrot, and the only nocturnal one. It can't fly, and it has peculiar and specific breeding requirements. These characteristics, in combination with the depredations of humans and introduced pests, make the kākāpō one of the world's rarest birds — just 127 birds are known to survive, on a handful of offshore islands.

People seem to be drawn to the kākāpō, with its rugby-ball shape, owl-like face and enquiring expression. Sell-out crowds gather in hushed delight to view the 'spokesbird' of the species, a non-breeding male called Sirocco who is toured to zoos and sanctuaries around the country to promote the conservation message. Sirocco, shown here, unflustered by the attention, stares back with the wisdom of ages, and solemnly eats grapes.

KERERŪ
Hemiphaga novaeseelandiae

A whoosh of wing-beats, and the bough of a kōwhai tree bends under the weight of a beautiful but somewhat ungainly pigeon. The New Zealand native wood pigeon, known as kererū, or kūkū or kūkupa in the north, looks almost too fat to fly — and, during the fruiting season of trees such as pūriri and karaka, sometimes it very nearly is.

Unlike many other native birds, the kererū isn't big on song; you are more likely to hear the rhythmic swoosh of its large wings as it flies overhead, or catch sight of its glossy white breast as it surveys its surroundings or plops from branch to branch. Like tūī, they have a tendency towards public intoxication; tempted by introduced fruit trees such as guava, they can gorge themselves on overripe, fermenting fruit and then drunkenly crash into windows or cars.

TREES WE LOVE

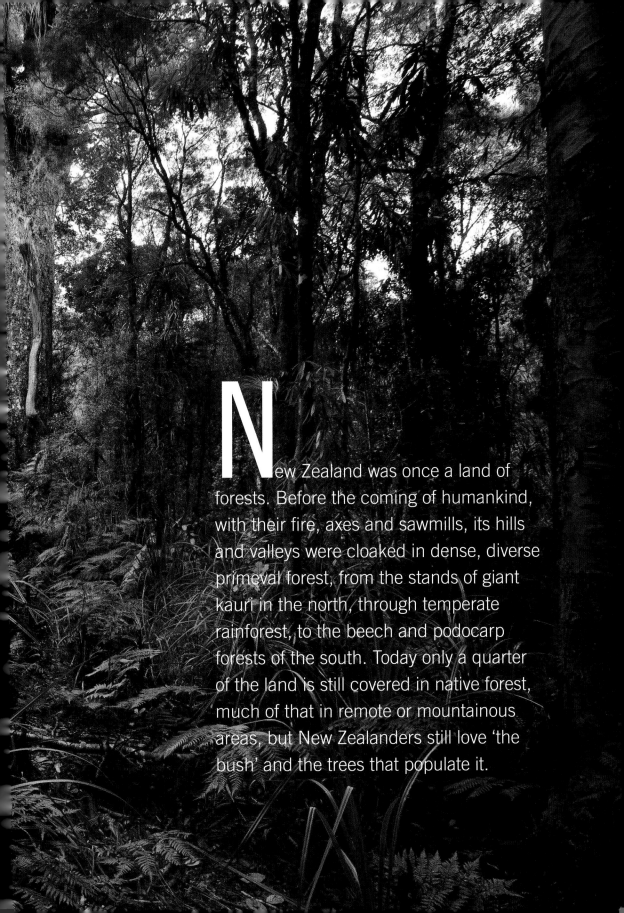

N

ew Zealand was once a land of
forests. Before the coming of humankind,
with their fire, axes and sawmills, its hills
and valleys were cloaked in dense, diverse
primeval forest, from the stands of giant
kauri in the north, through temperate
rainforest, to the beech and podocarp
forests of the south. Today only a quarter
of the land is still covered in native forest,
much of that in remote or mountainous
areas, but New Zealanders still love 'the
bush' and the trees that populate it.

PŌHUTUKAWA

Metrosideros excelsa

The flowering of the pōhutukawa is a sure sign that
summer is on the way, even if the windy spring has
not quite departed. All around the coastline of the
northern North Island, the shore turns blood-red
when the pōhutukawa bloom. Huge, gnarly trunks
and bendy branches make great places to climb and
hide, surrounded by the spiky red blooms which
fall to carpet the sand below. For the first European
settlers, homesick in a land where Christmas falls
in summertime, it became part of a new culture.
Those who settled further south were out of luck:
the pōhutukawa occurs naturally no further south
than Taranaki and Gisborne on the east and west
coasts, respectively.

KAURI
Agathis australis

Walking through a kauri forest is like stepping into a Gothic cathedral. Vast pale columns — not of stone, but of grey, hammered-looking bark — rise straight and true from the forest floor, branching into vaulted canopies tens of metres above. The greatest remaining tree, Tāne Mahuta, 'the Lord of the Forest', renders visitors to Waipoua Forest in Northland speechless, with his 51.5-metre height and 14-metre girth, but once he would have had many contemporaries.

One of the largest and oldest-growing trees in the world, the kauri was a victim of its own success. Once European explorers and entrepreneurs laid their eyes on the kauri forests, all they could see was the timber and the pounds sterling that it represented. Vast swathes of kauri, once covering 1.2 million hectares of land in Northland and the Coromandel Peninsula, were felled in the 1900s, its soft, golden timber turned into ships, spars, houses and furniture. Only pockets of it remain today, in protected parks where visitors can still come and worship.

CABBAGE TREE
Cordyline australis

This seems a humble sort of tree to love — a kind of scrubby outlier found on swampy, marginal farmland and silhouetted on rugged hills — but the cabbage tree, tī kōuka, is dear to many New Zealanders. It is instantly recognisable from its truffula-tree-like shape, with a long, straight trunk and a tufty bush of leaves at the top.

The tree got its name from the edible heart which lies at the centre of the leaves, eaten by Māori and early settlers alike. The fire-resistant trunk was also used for early cottage chimneys.

In spring the trees are fragrant with sprays of white flowers; a profuse early blooming is supposed to indicate a good summer ahead. Cabbage trees have also made good travellers; they are a surprisingly tropical feature of the southwest coast of England, where they are known as Torquay or Cornish palms.

RIMU
Dacrydium cupressinum

Rimu was a core species of the vast, ancient podocarp forests which once covered large areas of New Zealand. The arcades of ancient trees in the swamp forests of the South Island's west coast give an idea of what the primeval forests of the supercontinent Gondwanaland, from which New Zealand came, must have been like. You can be forgiven for thinking a browsing wetland dinosaur might appear from behind the moss-covered trunk of a giant rimu tree.

Unromantically called red pine by the first European settlers, rimu trees can live for 1000 years, and grow as high as 50 metres. Once a towering forest giant, many were reduced to furniture — like kauri, the beauty and versatility of its timber was rimu's ultimate downfall. Logging of this magnificent tree came to an end in 2000, and today its stronghold in the southwest is a World Heritage park.

SILVER FERN
Cyathea dealbata

The silver fern, or ponga, shines on the breast of the All Blacks and on the uniforms of our Olympians, just as it catches the light in the forest understorey. A common tree fern in New Zealand's temperate rainforests, the white underside of the leaves of the ponga or silver fern were used by Māori to mark trails, and it has come to be a national symbol. And not only the unfurled fern is an icon: one of the most recognisable of Māori symbols, the koru, as seen on the tailfins of Air New Zealand planes, represents the unfurling fronds at the heart of the fern.

The silver fern was first used as a national symbol by the New Zealand Natives rugby team — a mostly Māori team shored up with a few New Zealand-born Pākehā — when it toured Britain in 1888–89, and it is now our most recognisable national sporting symbol.

OUR SONGS

Māori musical tradition has combined with European influences to produce a distinctly 'Kiwi music', a tradition which includes a sing-along around the piano or guitar at family gatherings, rowdy summertime gigs at pubs around the country, and music festivals.

Not everyone knows the words to the verses — or even that there *is* more than one verse — but there aren't many Kiwis who couldn't join in on the chorus of 'Ten Guitars'. Written by Gordon Mills and originally recorded as a B-side to 'Release Me' by British singer Engelbert Humperdinck, 'Ten Guitars' was a radio hit in New Zealand in the 1960s. It became a popular singalong for Māori shearing gangs and at parties, with the addition of the 'Māori strum' guitar technique, which involves damping the strings with the palm after each strum to create a rhythm.

What you'll also catch us singing are songs by the Finn brothers, Tim and Neil. From their Split Enz and Crowded House days we'll launch into 'I See Red', 'Six Months in a Leaky Boat' or 'Weather With You'.

And we'll also sing goodbye. In 1935 Maewa Kaihau modified 'Pō Atarau', itself based on an earlier song which was sung to farewell Māori soldiers heading for battlefields of the First World War, into the 'Haere Rā Waltz', which New Zealanders would sing as they waved from the wharf to their relatives leaving on steamships for overseas.

In 1945 the famous English wartime singer Gracie Fields toured New Zealand, where she heard the 'Haere Rā Waltz'. Her version of it, 'Now Is The Hour', became a worldwide hit in 1948.

OUR
MOST FAMOUS
SHORT STORY

'At the Bay' was written by Katherine Mansfield in 1921. The setting is Days Bay, across the harbour from Wellington City, and the place where Mansfield spent summers in her childhood. Mansfield, who is regarded as one of the finest exponents of the short story in the English language, left New Zealand in 1908, when she was 19, and never returned, although her fondness for her country increased in the years before her premature death in 1923 at the age of 34. She was a contemporary of Virginia Woolf and DH Lawrence and was married to the publisher John Middleton Murry.

AT THE BAY
KATHERINE MANSFIELD

I /

Very early morning. The sun was not yet risen, and the whole of Crescent Bay was hidden under a white sea-mist. The big bush-covered hills at the back were smothered. You could not see where they ended and the paddocks and bungalows began. The sandy road was gone and the paddocks and bungalows the other side of it; there were no white dunes covered with reddish grass beyond them; there was nothing to mark which was beach and where was the sea. A heavy dew had fallen. The grass was blue. Big drops hung on the bushes and just did not fall; the silvery, fluffy toi-toi was limp on its long stalks, and all the marigolds and the pinks in the bungalow gardens were bowed to the earth with wetness. Drenched were the cold fuchsias, round pearls of dew lay on the flat nasturtium leaves. It looked as though the sea had beaten up softly in the darkness, as though one immense wave had come rippling, rippling — how far? Perhaps if you had waked up in the middle of the night you might have seen a big fish flicking in at the window and gone again. . . .

Ah-Aah! sounded the sleepy sea. And from the bush there came the sound of little streams flowing, quickly, lightly, slipping between the smooth stones, gushing into ferny basins and out again; and there was the splashing of big drops on large leaves, and something else — what was it? — a faint stirring and shaking, the snapping of a twig and then such silence that it seemed someone was listening.

Round the corner of Crescent

Bay, between the piled-up masses of broken rock, a flock of sheep came pattering. They were huddled together, a small, tossing, woolly mass, and their thin, stick-like legs trotted along quickly as if the cold and the quiet had frightened them. Behind them an old sheep-dog, his soaking paws covered with sand, ran along with his nose to the ground, but carelessly, as if thinking of something else. And then in the rocky gateway the shepherd himself appeared. He was a lean, upright old man, in a frieze coat that was covered with a web of tiny drops, velvet trousers tied under the knee, and a wideawake with a folded blue handkerchief round the brim. One hand was crammed into his belt, the other grasped a beautifully smooth yellow stick. And as he walked, taking his time, he kept up a very soft light whistling, an airy, far-away fluting that sounded mournful and tender. The old dog cut an ancient caper or two and then drew up sharp, ashamed of his levity, and walked a few dignified paces by his master's side. The sheep ran forward in little pattering rushes; they began to bleat, and ghostly flocks and herds answered them from under the sea. "Baa! Baaa!" For a time they seemed to be always on the same piece of ground. There ahead was stretched the sandy road with shallow puddles; the same soaking bushes showed on either side and the same shadowy palings. Then something immense came into view; an enormous shock-haired giant with his arms stretched out. It was the big gum-tree outside Mrs Stubbs's shop, and as they passed by there was a strong whiff of eucalyptus. And now big spots of light gleamed in the mist. The shepherd stopped whistling; he rubbed his red nose and wet beard on his wet sleeve and, screwing up his eyes, glanced in the direction of the sea. The sun was rising. It was marvellous how quickly the mist thinned, sped away, dissolved from the shallow plain, rolled up from the bush and was gone as if in a hurry to escape; big twists and curls jostled and shouldered each other as the silvery beams broadened. The far-away sky — a bright, pure blue — was reflected in the puddles, and the drops, swimming along the telegraph poles, flashed into points of light. Now the leaping, glittering sea was so bright it made one's eyes ache to look at it. The shepherd drew a pipe, the bowl as small as an acorn, out of his breast-pocket, fumbled for a chunk of speckled tobacco, pared off a few shavings and stuffed the bowl. He was a grave, fine-looking old man. As he lit up and the blue smoke wreathed his head, the dog, watching, looked proud of him.

"Baa! Baaa!" The sheep spread out into a fan. They were just clear of the summer colony before the first sleeper turned over and lifted a drowsy head; their cry sounded in the dreams of little children . . . who lifted their arms to drag down, to cuddle the darling little woolly lambs of sleep. Then the first inhabitant appeared; it was the Burnells' cat Florrie, sitting on the gatepost, far too early as usual, looking for their milk-girl. When she saw the old sheep-dog she sprang up quickly, arched her back, drew in her tabby head, and seemed to give a little fastidious shiver. "Ugh! What a coarse, revolting creature!" said Florrie. But the old sheep-dog, not looking up, waggled past, flinging out his legs from side to side. Only one of his ears twitched to prove that he saw, and thought her a silly young female.

The breeze of morning lifted in the bush and the smell of leaves and wet black earth mingled with the sharp smell of the sea. Myriads of birds were singing. A goldfinch flew over the shepherd's head and, perching on the tiptop of a spray, it turned to the sun, ruffling its small breast feathers. And now they had passed the fisherman's hut, passed the charred-looking little whare where Leila the milk-girl lived with her old Gran. The sheep strayed over a yellow swamp and Wag, the sheep-dog, padded after, rounded them up and headed them for the steeper, narrower rocky pass that led out of Crescent Bay and towards Daylight Cove. "Baa! Baaa!" Faint the cry came as they rocked along the fast-drying road. The shepherd put away his pipe, dropping it into his breast-pocket so that the little bowl hung over. And straightaway the soft airy whistling began again. Wag ran out along a ledge of rock after something that smelled, and ran back again disgusted. Then pushing, nudging, hurrying, the sheep rounded the bend and the shepherd followed after out of sight.

II /

A few moments later the back door of one of the bungalows opened, and a figure in a broad-striped bathing suit flung down the paddock, cleared the stile, rushed through the tussock grass into the hollow, staggered up the sandy hillock, and raced for dear life over the big porous stones, over the cold, wet pebbles, on to the hard sand that gleamed like oil. Splish-Splosh! Splish-Splosh! The water bubbled round his legs as Stanley Burnell waded out exulting. First man in as usual! He'd beaten them all again. And he swooped down to souse his head and neck.

"Hail, brother! All hail, Thou

Mighty One!" A velvety bass voice came booming over the water.

Great Scott! Damnation take it! Stanley lifted up to see a dark head bobbing far out and an arm lifted. It was Jonathan Trout — there before him! "Glorious morning!" sang the voice.

"Yes, very fine!" said Stanley briefly. Why the dickens didn't the fellow stick to his part of the sea? Why should he come barging over to this exact spot? Stanley gave a kick, a lunge and struck out, swimming overarm. But Jonathan was a match for him. Up he came, his black hair sleek on his forehead, his short beard sleek.

"I had an extraordinary dream last night!" he shouted.

What was the matter with the man? This mania for conversation irritated Stanley beyond words. And it was always the same, always some piffle about a dream he'd had, or some cranky idea he'd got hold of, or some rot he'd been reading. Stanley turned over on his back and kicked with his legs till he was a living waterspout. But even then . . . "I dreamed I was hanging over a terrifically high cliff, shouting to someone below." You would be! thought Stanley. He could stick no more of it. He stopped splashing. "Look here, Trout," he said, "I'm in rather a hurry this morning."

"You're *what*?" Jonathan was so surprised — or pretended to be — that he sank under the water, then reappeared again blowing.

"All I mean is," said Stanley, "I've no time to — to — to fool about. I want to get this over. I'm in a hurry. I've work to do this morning — see?"

Jonathan was gone before Stanley had finished. "Pass, friend!" said the bass voice gently, and he slid away through the water with scarcely a ripple . . . But curse the fellow! He'd ruined Stanley's bathe. What an unpractical idiot the man was! Stanley struck out to sea again, and then as quickly swam in again, and away he rushed up the beach. He felt cheated.

Jonathan stayed a little longer in the water. He floated, gently moving his hands like fins, and letting the sea rock his long, skinny body. It was curious, but in spite of everything he was fond of Stanley Burnell. True, he had a fiendish desire to tease him sometimes, to poke fun at him, but at bottom he was sorry for the fellow. There was something pathetic in his determination to make a job of everything. You couldn't help feeling he'd be caught out one day, and then what an almighty cropper he'd come! At that moment an immense wave lifted Jonathan, rode past him, and broke along the beach with a joyful sound. What a beauty! And now there came another. That was the way to live — carelessly, recklessly, spending oneself. He got on to his feet and began to wade towards the shore, pressing his toes into the firm, wrinkled sand. To take things easy, not to fight against the ebb and flow of life, but to give way to it — that was what was needed. It was this tension that was all wrong. To live — to live! And the perfect morning, so fresh and fair, basking in the light, as though laughing at its own beauty, seemed to whisper, "Why not?"

But now he was out of the water Jonathan turned blue with cold. He ached all over; it was as though someone was wringing the blood out of him. And stalking up the beach, shivering, all his muscles tight, he too felt his bathe was spoilt. He'd stayed in too long.

III /

Beryl was alone in the living-room when Stanley appeared, wearing a blue serge suit, a stiff collar and a spotted tie. He looked almost uncannily clean and brushed; he was going to town for the day. Dropping into his chair, he pulled out his watch and put it beside his plate.

"I've just got twenty-five minutes," he said. "You might go and see if the porridge is ready, Beryl?"

"Mother's just gone for it," said Beryl. She sat down at the table and poured out his tea.

"Thanks!" Stanley took a sip. "Hallo!" he said in an astonished voice, "you've forgotten the sugar."

"Oh, sorry!" But even then Beryl didn't help him; she pushed the basin across. What did this mean? As Stanley helped himself his blue eyes widened; they seemed to quiver. He shot a quick glance at his sister-in-law and leaned back.

"Nothing wrong, is there?" he asked carelessly, fingering his collar.

Beryl's head was bent; she turned her plate in her fingers.

"Nothing," said her light voice. Then she too looked up, and smiled at Stanley. "Why should there be?"

"O-oh! No reason at all as far as I know. I thought you seemed rather—"

At that moment the door opened and the three little girls appeared, each carrying a porridge plate. They were dressed alike in blue jerseys and knickers, their brown legs were bare, and each had her hair plaited and pinned up in what was called a horse's tail. Behind them came Mrs Fairfield with the tray.

"Carefully, children," she warned. But they were taking the very greatest care. They loved being allowed to carry things. "Have you said good-morning to your father?"

"Yes, grandma." They settled themselves on the bench opposite

Stanley and Beryl.

"Good morning, Stanley!" Old Mrs Fairfield gave him his plate.

"Morning, mother! How's the boy?"

"Splendid! He only woke up once last night. What a perfect morning!" The old woman paused, her hand on the loaf of bread, to gaze out of the open door into the garden. The sea sounded. Through the wide-open window streamed the sun on to the yellow varnished walls and bare floor. Everything on the table flashed and glittered. In the middle there was an old salad bowl filled with yellow and red nasturtiums. She smiled, and a look of deep content shone in her eyes.

"You might *cut* me a slice of that bread, mother," said Stanley. "I've only twelve and a half minutes before the coach passes. Has anyone given my shoes to the servant girl?"

"Yes, they're ready for you." Mrs Fairfield was quite unruffled.

"Oh, Kezia! Why are you such a messy child?" cried Beryl despairingly.

"Me, Aunt Beryl?" Kezia stared at her. What had she done now? She had only dug a river down the middle of her porridge, filled it, and was eating the banks away. But she did that every single morning, and no one had said a word up till now.

"Why can't you eat your food properly like Isabel and Lottie?" How unfair grown-ups are!

"But Lottie always makes a floating island, don't you, Lottie?"

"I don't," said Isabel smartly. "I just sprinkle mine with sugar and put on the milk and finish it. Only babies play with their food."

Stanley pushed back his chair and got up.

"Would you get me those shoes, mother? And, Beryl, if you've finished, I wish you'd cut down to the gate and stop the coach. Run in to your mother, Isabel, and ask her where my bowler hat's been put. Wait a minute — have you children been playing with my stick?"

"No, father!"

"But I put it here," Stanley began to bluster. "I remember distinctly putting it in this corner. Now, who's had it? There's no time to lose. Look sharp! The stick's got to be found."

Even Alice, the servant girl, was drawn into the chase. "You haven't been using it to poke the kitchen fire with by any chance?"

Stanley dashed into the bedroom where Linda was lying. "Most extraordinary thing. I can't keep a single possession to myself. They've made away with my stick, now!"

"Stick, dear? What stick?" Linda's vagueness on these occasions could not be real, Stanley decided. Would nobody sympathise with him?

"Coach! Coach, Stanley!" Beryl's voice cried from the gate.

Stanley waved his arm to Linda. "No time to say good-bye!" he cried. And he meant that as a punishment to her.

He snatched his bowler hat, dashed out of the house, and swung down the garden path. Yes, the coach was there waiting, and Beryl, leaning over the open gate, was laughing up at somebody or other just as if nothing had happened. The heartlessness of women! The way they took it for granted it was your job to slave away for them while they didn't even take the trouble to see that your walking-stick wasn't lost. Kelly trailed his whip across the horses.

"Good-bye, Stanley," called Beryl, sweetly and gaily. It was easy enough to say good-bye! And there she stood, idle, shading her eyes with her hand. The worst of it was Stanley had to shout good-bye too, for the sake of appearances. Then he saw her turn, give a little skip and run back to the house. She was glad to be rid of him!

Yes, she was thankful. Into the living-room she ran and called "He's gone!" Linda cried from her room: "Beryl! Has Stanley gone?" Old Mrs Fairfield appeared, carrying the boy in his little flannel coatee.

"Gone?"

"Gone!"

Oh, the relief, the difference it made to have the man out of the house. Their very voices were changed as they called to one another; they sounded warm and loving and as if they shared a secret. Beryl went over to the table. "Have another cup of tea, mother. It's still hot." She wanted, somehow, to celebrate the fact that they could do what they liked now. There was no man to disturb them; the whole perfect day was theirs.

"No, thank you, child," said old Mrs Fairfield, but the way at that moment she tossed the boy up and said "a-goos-a-goos a-ga!" to him meant that she felt the same. The little girls ran into the paddock like chickens let out of a coop.

Even Alice, the servant girl, washing up the dishes in the kitchen, caught the infection and used the precious tank water in a perfectly reckless fashion.

"Oh, these men!" said she, and she plunged the teapot into the bowl and held it under the water even after it had stopped bubbling, as if it too was a man and drowning was too good for them.

IV /

"Wait for me, Isa-bel! Kezia, wait for me!"

There was poor little Lottie, left behind again, because she found it so fearfully hard to get over the stile by herself. When she stood on the first step her knees began to wobble; she grasped the post. Then you had to put one leg over. But which leg? She never could decide. And when she did finally put one leg over with a sort of stamp of despair — then the feeling was awful. She was half in the paddock still and half in the tussock grass. She clutched the post desperately and lifted up her voice. "Wait for me!"

"No, don't you wait for her, Kezia!" said Isabel. "She's such a little silly. She's always making a fuss. Come on!" And she tugged Kezia's jersey. "You can use my bucket if you come with me," she said kindly "It's bigger than yours." But Kezia couldn't leave Lottie all by herself. She ran back to her. By this time Lottie was very red in the face and breathing heavily.

"Here, put your other foot over," said Kezia.

"Where?"

Lottie looked down at Kezia as if from a mountain height.

"Here where my hand is." Kezia patted the place.

"Oh, *there* do you mean?" Lottie gave a deep sigh and put the second foot over.

"Now — sort of turn round and sit down and slide," said Kezia.

"But there's nothing to sit down *on*, Kezia," said Lottie.

She managed it at last, and once it was over she shook herself and began to beam.

"I'm getting better at climbing over stiles, aren't I, Kezia?"

Lottie's was a very hopeful nature.

The pink and the blue sunbonnet followed Isabel's bright red sunbonnet up that sliding, slipping hill. At the top they paused to decide where to go and to have a good stare at who was there already. Seen from behind, standing against the sky line, gesticulating largely with their spades, they looked like minute puzzled explorers.

The whole family of Samuel Josephs was there already with their lady-help, who sat on a camp-stool and kept order with a whistle that she wore tied round her neck, and a small cane with which she directed operations. The Samuel Josephs never played by themselves or managed their own game. If they did, it ended in the boys pouring water down the girls' necks or the girls trying to put little black crabs into the boys' pockets. So Mrs S. J. and the poor lady-help drew up what she called a "brogramme" every morning to keep them "abused and out of bischief ". It was all competitions or races or round games. Everything began with a piercing blast of the lady-help's whistle and ended with another. There were even prizes — large, rather dirty paper parcels which the lady-help with a sour little smile drew out of a bulging string kit. The Samuel Josephs fought fearfully for the prizes and cheated and pinched one another's arms — they were all expert pinchers. The only time the Burnell children ever played with them Kezia had got a prize, and when she undid three bits of paper she found a very small rusty button-hook. She couldn't understand why they made such a fuss. . . .

But they never played with the Samuel Josephs now or even went to their parties. The Samuel Josephs were always giving children's parties at the Bay and there was always the same food. A big washhand basin of very brown fruit salad, buns cut into four and a washhand jug full of something the lady-help called "Limmonadear". And you went away in the evening with half the frill torn off your frock or something spilled all down the front of your open-work pinafore, leaving the Samuel Josephs leaping like savages on their lawn. No! They were too awful.

On the other side of the beach, close down to the water, two little boys, their knickers rolled up, twinkled like spiders. One was digging, the other pattered in and out of the water, filling a small bucket. They were the Trout boys, Pip and Rags. But Pip was so busy digging and Rags was so busy helping that they didn't see their little cousins until they were quite close.

"Look!" said Pip. "Look what I've discovered." And he showed them an old, wet, squashed-looking boot. The three little girls stared.

"Whatever are you going to do with it?" asked Kezia.

"Keep it, of course!" Pip was very scornful. "It's a find — see?"

Yes, Kezia saw that. All the same . . .

"There's lots of things buried in the sand," explained Pip.

"They get chucked up from wrecks. Treasure. Why — you might find—"

"But why does Rags have to keep on pouring water in?" asked Lottie.

"Oh, that's to moisten it," said Pip, "to make the work a bit easier. Keep it up, Rags." And good little Rags ran up and down, pouring in the water that turned brown like cocoa.

"Here, shall I show you what I found yesterday?" said Pip mysteriously, and he stuck his spade into the sand. "Promise not to tell."

They promised.

"Say, cross my heart straight dinkum."

The little girls said it.

Pip took something out of his pocket, rubbed it a long time on the front of his jersey, then breathed on it and rubbed it again.

"Now turn round!" he ordered.

They turned round.

"All look the same way! Keep still! Now!"

And his hand opened; he held up to

the light something that flashed, that winked, that was a most lovely green.

"It's a nemeral," said Pip solemnly.

"Is it really, Pip?" Even Isabel was impressed.

The lovely green thing seemed to dance in Pip's fingers. Aunt Beryl had a nemeral in a ring, but it was a very small one. This one was as big as a star and far more beautiful.

V /

As the morning lengthened whole parties appeared over the sand-hills and came down on the beach to bathe. It was understood that at eleven o'clock the women and children of the summer colony had the sea to themselves. First the women undressed, pulled on their bathing dresses and covered their heads in hideous caps like sponge-bags; then the children were unbuttoned. The beach was strewn with little heaps of clothes and shoes; the big summer hats, with stones on them to keep them from blowing away, looked like immense shells. It was strange that even the sea seemed to sound differently when all those leaping, laughing figures ran into the waves. Old Mrs Fairfield, in a lilac cotton dress and a black hat tied under the chin, gathered her little

brood and got them ready. The little Trout boys whipped their shirts over their heads, and away the five sped, while their grandma sat with one hand in her knitting-bag ready to draw out the ball of wool when she was satisfied they were safely in.

The firm compact little girls were not half so brave as the tender, delicate-looking little boys. Pip and Rags, shivering, crouching down, slapping the water, never hesitated. But Isabel, who could swim twelve strokes, and Kezia, who could nearly swim eight, only followed on the strict understanding they were not to be splashed. As for Lottie, she didn't follow at all. She liked to be left to go in her own way, please. And that way was to sit down at the edge of the water, her legs straight, her knees pressed together, and to make vague motions with her arms as if she expected to be wafted out to sea. But when a bigger wave than usual, an old whiskery one, came lolloping along in her direction, she scrambled to her feet with a face of horror and flew up the beach again.

"Here, mother, keep these for me, will you?"

Two rings and a thin gold chain were dropped into Mrs Fairfield's lap. "Yes, dear. But aren't you going to bathe here?"

"No-o," Beryl drawled. She sounded vague. "I'm undressing

farther along. I'm going to bathe with Mrs Harry Kember."

"Very well." But Mrs Fairfield's lips set. She disapproved of Mrs Harry Kember. Beryl knew it.

Poor old mother, she smiled as she skimmed over the stones. Poor old mother! Old! Oh, what joy, what bliss it was to be young. . . .

"You look very pleased," said Mrs Harry Kember. She sat hunched up on the stones, her arms round her knees, smoking.

"It's such a lovely day," said Beryl, smiling down at her.

"Oh, my *dear*!" Mrs Harry Kember's voice sounded as though she knew better than that. But then her voice always sounded as though she knew something more about you than you did yourself. She was a long, strange-looking woman with narrow hands and feet. Her face, too, was long and narrow and exhausted-looking; even her fair curled fringe looked burnt out and withered. She was the only woman at the Bay who smoked, and she smoked incessantly, keeping the cigarette between her lips while she talked, and only taking it out when the ash was so long you could not understand why it did not fall. When she was not playing bridge — she played bridge every day of her life — she spent her time lying in the full glare of the sun. She could stand any amount of it; she

never had enough. All the same, it did not seem to warm her. Parched, withered, cold, she lay stretched on the stones like a piece of tossed-up driftwood. The women at the Bay thought she was very, very fast. Her lack of vanity, her slang, the way she treated men as though she was one of them, and the fact that she didn't care twopence about her house and called the servant Gladys "Glad-eyes", was disgraceful. Standing on the verandah steps Mrs Kember would call in her indifferent, tired voice, "I say, Glad-eyes, you might heave me a handkerchief if I've got one, will you?" And Glad-eyes, a red bow in her hair instead of a cap, and white shoes, came running with an impudent smile. It was an absolute scandal! True, she had no children, and her husband . . . Here the voices were always raised; they became fervent. How can he have married her? How can he, how can he? It must have been money, of course, but even then!

Mrs Kember's husband was at least ten years younger than she was, and so incredibly handsome that he looked like a mask or a most perfect illustration in an American novel rather than a man. Black hair, dark blue eyes, red lips, a slow sleepy smile, a fine tennis player, a perfect dancer, and with it all a mystery. Harry Kember was like a man walking in his sleep. Men couldn't stand him, they couldn't get a word out of the chap; he ignored his wife just as she ignored him. How did he live? Of course there were stories, but such stories! They simply couldn't be told. The women he'd been seen with, the places he'd been seen in . . . but nothing was ever certain, nothing definite. Some of the women at the Bay privately thought he'd commit a murder one day. Yes, even while they talked to Mrs Kember and took in the awful concoction she was wearing, they saw her, stretched as she lay on the beach; but cold, bloody and still with a cigarette stuck in the corner of her mouth.

Mrs Kember rose, yawned, unsnapped her belt buckle, and tugged at the tape of her blouse. And Beryl stepped out of her skirt and shed her jersey, and stood up in her short white petticoat, and her camisole with ribbon bows on the shoulders.

"Mercy on us," said Mrs Harry Kember, "what a little beauty you are!'

"Don't!" said Beryl softly; but, drawing off one stocking and then the other, she felt a little beauty.

"My dear — why not?" said Mrs Harry Kember, stamping on her own petticoat. Really — her underclothes! A pair of blue cotton knickers and a linen bodice that reminded one somehow of a pillow-case. . . . "And you don't wear stays, do you?" She

touched Beryl's waist, and Beryl sprang away with a small affected cry. Then "Never!" she said firmly.

"Lucky little creature," sighed Mrs Kember, unfastening her own.

Beryl turned her back and began the complicated movements of someone who is trying to take off her clothes and to pull on her bathing-dress all at one and the same time.

"Oh, my dear — don't mind me," said Mrs Harry Kember. "Why be shy? I shan't eat you. I shan't be shocked like those other ninnies." And she gave her strange neighing laugh and grimaced at the other women.

But Beryl was shy. She never undressed in front of anybody. Was that silly? Mrs Harry Kember made her feel it was silly, even something to be ashamed of. Why be shy indeed! She glanced quickly at her friend standing so boldly in her torn chemise and lighting a fresh cigarette; and a quick, bold, evil feeling started up in her breast. Laughing recklessly, she drew on the limp, sandy-feeling bathing-dress that was not quite dry and fastened the twisted buttons.

"That's better," said Mrs Harry Kember. They began to go down the beach together. "Really, it's a sin for you to wear clothes, my dear. Somebody's got to tell you some day."

The water was quite warm. It was that marvellous transparent blue, flecked with silver, but the sand at the bottom looked gold; when you kicked with your toes there rose a little puff of gold-dust. Now the waves just reached her breast. Beryl stood, her arms outstretched, gazing out, and as each wave came she gave the slightest little jump, so that it seemed it was the wave which lifted her so gently.

"I believe in pretty girls having a good time," said Mrs Harry Kember. "Why not? Don't you make a mistake, my dear. Enjoy yourself." And suddenly she turned turtle, disappeared, and swam away quickly, quickly, like a rat. Then she flicked round and began swimming back. She was going to say something else. Beryl felt that she was being poisoned by this cold woman, but she longed to hear. But oh, how strange, how horrible! As Mrs Harry Kember came up close she looked, in her black waterproof bathing-cap, with her sleepy face lifted above the water, just her chin touching, like a horrible caricature of her husband.

VI /

In a steamer chair, under a manuka tree that grew in the middle of the front grass patch, Linda Burnell dreamed the morning away. She did nothing. She looked up the dark, close, dry leaves of the manuka, at the chinks of blue between, and now and again a tiny yellowish flower dropped on her. Pretty — yes, if you held one of those flowers on the palm of your hand and looked at it closely, it was an exquisite small thing. Each pale yellow petal shone as if each was the careful work of a loving hand. The tiny tongue in the centre gave it the shape of a bell. And when you turned it over the outside was a deep bronze colour. But as soon as they flowered, they fell and were scattered. You brushed them off your frock as you talked; the horrid little things got caught in one's hair. Why, then, flower at all? Who takes the trouble — or the joy — to make all these things that are wasted, wasted. . . . It was uncanny.

On the grass beside her, lying between two pillows, was the boy. Sound asleep he lay, his head turned away from his mother. His fine dark hair looked more like a shadow than like real hair, but his ear was a bright, deep coral. Linda clasped her hands above her head and crossed her feet. It was very pleasant to know that all these bungalows were empty, that everybody was down on the beach, out of sight, out of hearing. She had the garden to herself; she was alone.

Dazzling white the picotees shone; the golden-eyed marigolds glittered; the nasturtiums wreathed the verandah poles in green and gold flame. If only one had time to look at these flowers long enough, time to get over the sense of novelty and strangeness, time to know them! But as soon as one paused to part the petals, to discover the under-side of the leaf, along came Life and one was swept away. And, lying in her cane chair, Linda felt so light; she felt like a leaf. Along came Life like a wind and she was seized and shaken; she had to go. Oh dear, would it always be so? Was there no escape?

. . . Now she sat on the verandah of their Tasmanian home, leaning against her father's knee. And he promised, "As soon as you and I are old enough, Linny, we'll cut off somewhere, we'll escape. Two boys together. I have a fancy I'd like to sail up a river in China." Linda saw that river, very wide, covered with little rafts and boats. She saw the yellow hats of the boatmen and she heard their high, thin voices as they called . . .

"Yes, papa."

But just then a very broad young man with bright ginger hair walked slowly past their house, and slowly, solemnly even, uncovered. Linda's father pulled her ear teasingly in the way he had.

"Linny's beau," he whispered.

"Oh, papa, fancy being married to Stanley Burnell!"

Well, she was married to him. And what was more she loved him. Not the Stanley whom everyone saw, not the everyday one; but a timid, sensitive, innocent Stanley who knelt down every night to say his prayers, and who longed to be good. Stanley was simple. If he believed in people — as he believed in her, for instance — it was with his whole heart. He could not be disloyal; he could not tell a lie. And how terribly he suffered if he thought anyone — she — was not being dead straight, dead sincere with him!

"This is too subtle for me!" He flung out the words, but his open, quivering, distraught look was like the look of a trapped beast.

But the trouble was — here Linda felt almost inclined to laugh, though heaven knows it was no laughing matter — she saw her Stanley so seldom. There were glimpses, moments, breathing spaces of calm, but all the rest of the time it was like living in a house that couldn't be cured of the habit of catching on fire, or a ship that got wrecked every day. And it was always Stanley who was in the thick of the danger. Her whole time was spent in rescuing him, and restoring him, and calming him down, and listening to his story. And what was left of her time spent in the dread of having children.

Linda frowned; she sat up quickly in her steamer chair and clasped her ankles. Yes, that was her real grudge against life; that was what she could not understand. That was the question she asked and asked, and listened in vain for the answer. It was all very well to say it was the common lot of women to bear children. It wasn't true. She, for one, could prove that wrong. She was broken, made weak, her courage was gone, through child-bearing. And what made it doubly hard to bear was, she did not love her children. It was useless pretending. Even if she had had the strength she never would have nursed and played with the little girls. No, it was as though a cold breath had chilled her through and through on each of those awful journeys; she had no warmth left to give them. As to the boy — well, thank heaven, mother had taken him; he was mother's, or Beryl's, or anybody's who wanted him. She had hardly held him in her arms. She was so indifferent about him, that as he lay there . . . Linda glanced down.

The boy had turned over. He lay facing her, and he was no longer asleep. His dark-blue, baby eyes were open; he looked as though he was peeping at his mother. And suddenly his face dimpled; it broke into a wide, toothless smile, a perfect beam, no less.

"I'm here!" that happy smile seemed to say. "Why don't you like *me*?"

There was something so quaint, so unexpected about that smile that Linda smiled herself. But she checked herself and said to the boy coldly, "I don't like babies."

"Don't like babies?" The boy couldn't believe her. "Don't like *me*?" He waved his arms foolishly at his mother.

Linda dropped off her chair on to the grass.

"Why do you keep on smiling?" she said severely. "If you knew what I was thinking about, you wouldn't."

But he only squeezed up his eyes, slyly, and rolled his head on the pillow. He didn't believe a word she said.

"We know all about that!" smiled the boy.

Linda was so astonished at the confidence of this little creature. . . . Ah no, be sincere. That was not what she felt; it was something far different, it was something so new, so . . . The tears danced in her eyes; she breathed in a small whisper to the boy, "Hallo, my funny!"

But by now the boy had forgotten his mother. He was serious again. Something pink, something soft waved in front of him. He made a grab at it and it immediately disappeared. But when he lay back, another, like the first, appeared. This time he determined to catch it. He made a tremendous effort and rolled right over.

VII /

The tide was out; the beach was deserted; lazily flopped the warm sea. The sun beat down, beat down hot and fiery on the fine sand, baking the grey and blue and black and white-veined pebbles. It sucked up the little drop of water that lay in the hollow of the curved shells; it bleached the pink convolvulus that threaded through and through the sand-hills. Nothing seemed to move but the small sand-hoppers. Pit-pit-pit! They were never still.

Over there on the weed-hung rocks that looked at low tide like shaggy beasts come down to the water to drink, the sunlight seemed to spin like a silver coin dropped into each of the small rock pools. They danced, they quivered, and minute ripples laved the porous shores. Looking down, bending over, each pool was like a lake with pink and blue houses clustered on the shores; and oh! the vast mountainous country behind those houses — the ravines, the passes, the dangerous creeks and fearful tracks that led to the water's edge. Underneath waved the sea-forest — pink thread-like trees, velvet anemones, and orange berry-spotted weeds. Now a stone on the bottom moved, rocked, and there was a glimpse of a black feeler; now a threadlike creature wavered by and was lost. Something was happening to the pink waving trees; they were changing to a cold moonlight blue. And now there sounded the faintest "plop". Who made that sound? What was going on down there? And how strong, how damp the seaweed smelt in the hot sun. . . .

The green blinds were drawn in the bungalows of the summer colony. Over the verandahs, prone on the paddock, flung over the fences, there were exhausted-looking bathing-dresses and rough striped towels. Each back window seemed to have a pair of sand-shoes on the sill and some lumps of rock or a bucket or a collection of pawa shells. The bush quivered in a haze of heat; the sandy road was empty except for the Trouts' dog Snooker, who lay stretched in the very middle of it. His blue eye was turned up, his legs stuck out stiffly, and he gave an occasional desperate-sounding puff, as much as to say he had decided to make an end of it and was only waiting for some kind cart to come along.

"What are you looking at, my grandma? Why do you keep stopping and sort of staring at the wall?"

Kezia and her grandmother were taking their siesta together. The little girl, wearing only her short drawers and her under-bodice, her arms and legs bare, lay on one of the puffed-up pillows of her grandma's bed, and the old woman, in a white ruffled dressing-gown, sat in a rocker at the window, with a long piece of pink knitting in her lap. This room that they shared, like the other rooms of the bungalow, was of light varnished wood and the floor was bare. The furniture was of the shabbiest, the simplest. The dressing-table for instance, was a packing-case in a sprigged muslin petticoat, and the mirror above was very strange; it was as though a little piece of forked lightning was imprisoned in it. On the table there stood a jar of sea-pinks, pressed so tightly together they looked more like a velvet pin-cushion, and a special shell which Kezia had given her grandma for a pin-tray, and another even more special which she had thought would make a very nice place for a watch to curl up in.

"Tell me, grandma," said Kezia.

The old woman sighed, whipped the wool twice round her thumb, and drew the bone needle through. She was casting on.

"I was thinking of your Uncle William, darling," she said quietly.

"My Australian Uncle William?" said Kezia. She had another.

"Yes, of course."

"The one I never saw?"

"That was the one."

"Well, what happened to him?" Kezia knew perfectly well, but she wanted to be told again.

"He went to the mines, and he got a sunstroke there and died," said old Mrs Fairfield.

Kezia blinked and considered the picture again. . . . A little man fallen over like a tin soldier by the side of a big black hole.

"Does it make you sad to think about him, grandma?" She hated her grandma to be sad.

It was the old woman's turn to consider. Did it make her sad? To look back, back. To stare down the years, as Kezia had seen her doing. To look after *them* as a woman does, long after *they* were out of sight. Did it make her sad? No, life was like that.

"No, Kezia."

"But why?" asked Kezia. She lifted one bare arm and began to draw things in the air. "Why did Uncle William have to die? He wasn't old."

Mrs Fairfield began counting the stitches in threes. "It just happened," she said in an absorbed voice.

"Does everybody have to die?" asked Kezia.

"Everybody!"

"*Me?*" Kezia sounded fearfully incredulous.

"Some day, my darling."

"But, grandma." Kezia waved her left leg and waggled the toes. They felt sandy. "What if I just won't?"

The old woman sighed again and drew a long thread from the ball.

"We're not asked, Kezia," she said sadly. "It happens to all of us sooner or later."

Kezia lay still thinking this over. She didn't want to die. It meant she would have to leave here, leave everywhere, for ever, leave — leave her grandma. She rolled over quickly.

"Grandma," she said in a startled voice.

"What, my pet!"

"*You're* not to die." Kezia was very decided.

"Ah, Kezia" — her grandma looked up and smiled and shook her head — "don't let's talk about it."

"But you're not to. You couldn't leave me. You couldn't not be there." This was awful. "Promise me you won't ever do it, grandma," pleaded Kezia.

The old woman went on knitting.

"Promise me! Say never!"

But still her grandma was silent.

Kezia rolled off the bed; she couldn't bear it any longer, and lightly she leapt on to her grandma's knees, clasped her hands round the old woman's throat and began kissing her, under the chin, behind the ear, and blowing down her neck.

"Say never . . . say never . . . say never—" She gasped between the kisses. And then she began, very softly and lightly, to tickle her grandma.

"Kezia!" The old woman dropped her knitting. She swung back in the rocker. She began to tickle Kezia. "Say never, say never, say never," gurgled Kezia, while they lay there laughing in each other's arms. "Come, that's enough, my squirrel! That's enough, my wild pony!" said old Mrs Fairfield, setting her cap straight. "Pick up my knitting."

Both of them had forgotten what the "never" was about.

VIII /

The sun was still full on the garden when the back door of the Burnells' shut with a bang and a very gay figure walked down the path to the gate. It was Alice, the servant-girl, dressed for her afternoon out. She wore a white cotton dress with such large red spots on it, and so many that they made you shudder, white shoes and a leghorn turned up under the brim with poppies. Of course she wore gloves, white ones, stained at the fastenings with iron-mould, and in one hand she carried a very dashed-looking sunshade which she referred to as her *perishall*.

Beryl, sitting in the window, fanning her freshly washed hair, thought she had never seen such a guy. If Alice had only blacked her face with a piece of cork before she started out, the picture would have been complete. And where did a girl like that go to in a place like this? The heart-shaped Fijian fan beat scornfully at that lovely bright mane. She supposed Alice had picked up some horrible common larrikin and they'd go off into the bush together. Pity to make herself so conspicuous; they'd have hard work to hide with Alice in that rig-out.

But no, Beryl was unfair. Alice was going to tea with Mrs Stubbs, who'd sent her an "invite" by the little boy who called for orders. She had taken ever such a liking to Mrs Stubbs ever since the first time she went to the shop to get something for her mosquitoes.

"Dear heart!" Mrs Stubbs had clapped her hand to her side. "I never seen anyone so eaten. You might have been attacked by canningbals."

Alice did wish there'd been a bit of life on the road though. Made her feel so queer, having nobody behind her. Made her feel all weak in the spine. She couldn't believe that someone wasn't watching her. And yet it was silly to turn round; it gave you away. She pulled up her gloves, hummed to herself and said to the distant gum tree, "Shan't be long now." But that was hardly company.

Mrs Stubbs's shop was perched on a little hillock just off the road. It had two big windows for eyes, a broad verandah for a hat, and the sign on the roof, scrawled MRS STUBBS'S, was like a little card stuck rakishly in the hat crown.

On the verandah there hung a long string of bathing-dresses, clinging together as though they'd just been rescued from the sea rather than waiting to go in, and beside them there hung a cluster of sand-shoes so extraordinarily mixed that to get at one pair you had to tear apart and forcibly separate at least fifty. Even then it was the rarest thing to find the left that belonged to the right. So many people had lost patience and gone off with one shoe that fitted and one that was a little too big. . . . Mrs Stubbs prided herself on keeping something of everything. The two windows, arranged in the form of precarious pyramids, were crammed so tight, piled so high, that it seemed only a conjuror could prevent them from toppling over. In the left-hand corner of one window, glued to the pane by four gelatine lozenges, there was — and there had been from time immemorial — a notice:

Lost! Hansome gole brooch
Solid gold
On or near beach
Reward offered

Alice pressed open the door. The bell jangled, the red serge curtains parted, and Mrs Stubbs appeared. With her broad smile and the long bacon knife in her hand she looked like a friendly brigand. Alice was welcomed so warmly that she found it quite difficult to keep up her "manners". They consisted of persistent little coughs and hems, pulls at her gloves, tweaks at her skirt, and a curious difficulty in seeing what was set before her or understanding what was said.

Tea was laid on the parlour table — ham, sardines, a whole pound of butter, and such a large johnny cake that it looked like an advertisement for somebody's baking powder. But the Primus stove roared so loudly that it was useless to try to talk above it. Alice sat down on the edge of a basket-chair while Mrs Stubbs pumped the stove still higher. Suddenly Mrs Stubbs whipped the cushion off a chair and disclosed a large brown-paper parcel.

"I've just had some new photers taken, my dear," she shouted cheerfully to Alice. "Tell me what you think of them."

In a very dainty, refined way Alice wet her finger and put the tissue back from the first one. Life! How many there were! There were three dozzing at least. And she held hers up to the light.

Mrs Stubbs sat in an arm-chair, leaning very much to one side. There was a look of mild astonishment on her large face, and well there might be. For though the arm-chair stood on a carpet, to the left of it, miraculously skirting the carpet border, there was a dashing waterfall. On her right stood a Grecian pillar with a giant fern tree on either side of it, and in the background towered a gaunt mountain, pale with snow.

"It is a nice style, isn't it?" shouted Mrs Stubbs; and Alice had just screamed "Sweetly" when the roaring of the Primus stove died down, fizzled out, ceased, and she said "Pretty" in a silence that was frightening.

"Draw up your chair, my dear," said Mrs Stubbs, beginning to pour out. "Yes," she said thoughtfully, as she handed the tea, "but I don't care about the size. I'm having an enlargemint. All very well for Christmas cards, but I never was the one for small photers myself. You get no comfort out of them. To say the truth, I find them dis'eartening."

Alice quite saw what she meant.

"Size," said Mrs Stubbs. "Give me size. That was what my poor dear husband was always saying. He couldn't stand anything small. Gave him the creeps. And, strange as it may seem, my dear" — here Mrs Stubbs creaked and seemed to expand herself at the memory — "it was dropsy that carried him off at the larst. Many's the time they drawn one and a half pints from 'im at the 'ospital. . . . it seemed like a judgmint."

Alice burned to know exactly what

it was that was drawn from him. She ventured, "I suppose it was water."

But Mrs Stubbs fixed Alice with her eyes and replied meaningly, "It was *liquid*, my dear."

Liquid! Alice jumped away from the word like a cat and came back to it, nosing and wary.

"That's 'im!" said Mrs Stubbs, and she pointed dramatically to the life-size head and shoulders of a burly man with a dead white rose in the button-hole of his coat that made you think of a curl of cold mutton fat. Just below, in silver letters on a red cardboard ground, were the words, "Be not afraid, it is I."

"It's ever such a fine face," said Alice faintly.

The pale-blue bow on the top of Mrs Stubbs's fair frizzy hair quivered. She arched her plump neck. What a neck she had! It was bright pink where it began and then it changed to warm apricot, and that faded to the colour of a brown egg and then to a deep creamy.

"All the same, my dear," she said surprisingly, "freedom's best!" Her soft, fat chuckle sounded like a purr. "Freedom's best," said Mrs Stubbs again.

Freedom! Alice gave a loud, silly little titter. She felt awkward. Her mind flew back to her own kitching. Ever so queer! She wanted to be back in it again.

IX /

A strange company assembled in the Burnells' washhouse after tea. Round the table there sat a bull, a rooster, a donkey that kept forgetting it was a donkey, a sheep and a bee. The washhouse was the perfect place for such a meeting because they could make as much noise as they liked and nobody ever interrupted. It was a small tin shed standing apart from the bungalow. Against the wall there was a deep trough and in the corner a copper with a basket of clothes-pegs on top of it. The little window, spun over with cobwebs, had a piece of candle and a mouse-trap on the dusty sill. There were clothes lines criss-crossed overhead and, hanging from a peg on the wall, a very big, a huge, rusty horseshoe. The table was in the middle with a form at either side.

"You can't be a bee, Kezia. A bee's not an animal. It's a ninseck."

"Oh, but I do want to be a bee frightfully," wailed Kezia. . . . A tiny bee, all yellow-furry, with striped legs. She drew her legs up under her and leaned over the table. She felt she was a bee.

"A ninseck must be an animal," she said stoutly. "It makes a noise. It's not like a fish."

"I'm a bull, I'm a bull!" cried Pip. And he gave such a tremendous bellow — how did he make that noise? — that Lottie looked quite alarmed.

"I'll be a sheep," said little Rags. "A whole lot of sheep went past this morning."

"How do you know?"

"Dad heard them. Baa!" He sounded like the little lamb that trots behind and seems to wait to be carried.

"Cock-a-doodle-do!" shrilled Isabel. With her red cheeks and bright eyes she looked like a rooster.

"What'll I be?" Lottie asked everybody, and she sat there smiling, waiting for them to decide for her. It had to be an easy one.

"Be a donkey, Lottie." It was Kezia's suggestion. "Hee-haw! You can't forget that."

"Hee-haw!" said Lottie solemnly. "When do I have to say it?"

"I'll explain, I'll explain," said the bull. It was he who had the cards. He waved them round his head. "All be quiet! All listen!" And he waited for them. "Look here, Lottie." He turned up a card. "It's got two spots on it — see? Now, if you put that card in the middle and somebody else has one with two spots as well, you say 'Hee-haw', and the card's yours."

"Mine?" Lottie was round-eyed. "To keep?"

"No, silly. Just for the game, see? Just while we're playing." The bull was very cross with her.

"Oh, Lottie, you *are* a little silly," said the proud rooster.

Lottie looked at both of them. Then she hung her head; her lip quivered. "I don't not want to play," she whispered. The others glanced at one another like conspirators. All of them knew what that meant. She would go away and be discovered somewhere standing with her pinny thrown over her head, in a corner, or against a wall, or even behind a chair.

"Yes, you *do*, Lottie. It's quite easy," said Kezia.

And Isabel, repentant, said exactly like a grown-up, "Watch *me*, Lottie, and you'll soon learn."

"Cheer up, Lot," said Pip. "There, I know what I'll do. I'll give you the first one. It's mine, really, but I'll give it to you. Here you are." And he slammed the card down in front of Lottie.

Lottie revived at that. But now she was in another difficulty. "I haven't got a hanky," she said; "I want one badly, too."

"Here, Lottie, you can use mine." Rags dipped into his sailor blouse and brought up a very wet-looking one, knotted together. "Be very careful," he warned her. "Only use that corner. Don't undo it. I've got a little starfish inside I'm going to try and tame."

"Oh, come on, you girls," said the bull. "And mind — you're not to look at your cards. You've got to keep your hands under the table till I say 'Go'."

Smack went the cards round the table. They tried with all their might to see, but Pip was too quick for them. It was very exciting, sitting there in the washhouse; it was all they could do not to burst into a little chorus of animals before Pip had finished dealing.

"Now, Lottie, you begin."

Timidly Lottie stretched out a hand, took the top card off her pack, had a good look at it — it was plain she was counting the spots — and put it down.

"No, Lottie, you can't do that. You mustn't look first. You must turn it the other way over."

"But then everybody will see it the same time as me," said Lottie.

The game proceeded. Mooe-ooo-er! The bull was terrible. He charged over the table and seemed to eat the cards up.

Bss-ss! said the bee.

Cock-a-doodle-do! Isabel stood up in her excitement and moved her elbows like wings.

Baa! Little Rags put down the King of Diamonds and Lottie put down the one they called the King of Spain. She had hardly any cards left.

"Why don't you call out, Lottie?"

"I've forgotten what I am," said the donkey woefully.

"Well, change! Be a dog instead! Bow-wow!"

"Oh yes. That's *much* easier."

Lottie smiled again. But when she and Kezia both had one Kezia waited on purpose. The others made signs to Lottie and pointed. Lottie turned very red; she looked bewildered, and at last she said, "Hee-haw! Kezia."

"Ss! Wait a minute!" They were in the very thick of it when the bull stopped them, holding up his hand. "What's that? What's that noise?"

"What noise? What do you mean?" asked the rooster.

"Ss! Shut up! Listen!" They were mouse-still. "I thought I heard a — a sort of knocking," said the bull.

"What was it like?" asked the sheep faintly.

No answer.

The bee gave a shudder. "Whatever did we shut the door for?" she said softly. Oh, why, why had they shut the door?

While they were playing, the day had faded; the gorgeous sunset had blazed and died. And now the quick dark came racing over the sea, over the sand-hills, up the paddock. You were frightened to look in the corners of the washhouse, and yet you had to look with all your might. And somewhere, far away, grandma was lighting a lamp. The blinds were being pulled down; the kitchen fire leapt in the tins on the mantelpiece.

"It would be awful now," said the bull, "if a spider was to fall from the ceiling on to the table, wouldn't it?"

"Spiders don't fall from ceilings."

"Yes, they do. Our Min told us she'd seen a spider as big as a saucer, with long hairs on it like a gooseberry."

Quickly all the little heads were jerked up; all the little bodies drew together, pressed together.

"Why doesn't somebody come and call us?" cried the rooster.

Oh, those grown-ups, laughing and snug, sitting in the lamp-light, drinking out of cups! They'd forgotten about them. No, not really forgotten. That was what their smile meant. They had decided to leave them there all by themselves.

Suddenly Lottie gave such a piercing scream that all of them jumped off the forms, all of them screamed too. "A face — a face looking!" shrieked Lottie.

It was true, it was real. Pressed against the window was a pale face, black eyes, a black beard.

"Grandma! Mother! Somebody!"

But they had not got to the door, tumbling over one another, before it opened for Uncle Jonathan. He had come to take the little boys home.

X /

He had meant to be there before, but in the front garden he had come upon Linda walking up and down the grass, stopping to pick off a dead pink or give a top-heavy carnation something to lean against, or to take a deep breath of something, and then walking on again, with her little air of remoteness. Over her white frock she wore a yellow, pink-fringed shawl from the Chinaman's shop.

"Hallo, Jonathan!" called Linda. And Jonathan whipped off his shabby panama, pressed it against his breast, dropped on one knee, and kissed Linda's hand.

"Greeting, my Fair One! Greeting, my Celestial Peach Blossom!" boomed the bass voice gently. "Where are the other noble dames?"

"Beryl's out playing bridge and mother's giving the boy his bath. . . . Have you come to borrow something?"

The Trouts were for ever running out of things and sending across to the Burnells' at the last moment.

But Jonathan only answered, "A little love, a little kindness"; and he walked by his sister-in-law's side.

Linda dropped into Beryl's hammock under the manuka tree and Jonathan stretched himself on the grass beside her, pulled a long stalk and began chewing it.

They knew each other well. The voices of children cried from the other gardens. A fisherman's light cart shook along the sandy road, and from far away they heard a dog barking; it was muffled as though the dog had its head in a sack. If you listened you could just hear the soft swish of the sea at full tide sweeping the pebbles. The sun was sinking.

"And so you go back to the office on Monday, do you, Jonathan?" asked Linda.

"On Monday the cage door opens and clangs to upon the victim for another eleven months and a week," answered Jonathan.

Linda swung a little. "It must be awful," she said slowly.

"Would ye have me laugh, my fair sister? Would ye have me weep?"

Linda was so accustomed to Jonathan's way of talking that she paid no attention to it.

"I suppose," she said vaguely, "one gets used to it. One gets used to anything."

"Does one? Hum!" The "Hum" was so deep it seemed to boom from underneath the ground. "I wonder how it's done," brooded Jonathan; "I've never managed it."

Looking at him as he lay there, Linda thought again how attractive he was. It was strange to think that he was only an ordinary clerk, that Stanley earned twice as much money as he. What was the matter with Jonathan? He had no ambition; she supposed that was it. And yet one felt he was gifted, exceptional. He was passionately fond of music; every spare penny he had went on books. He was always full of new ideas, schemes, plans. But nothing came of it all. The new fire blazed in Jonathan; you almost heard it roaring softly as he explained, described and dilated on the new thing; but a moment later it had fallen in and there was nothing but ashes, and Jonathan went about with a look like hunger in his black eyes. At these times he exaggerated his absurd manner of speaking, and he sang in church — he was the leader of the choir — with such fearful dramatic intensity that the meanest hymn put on an unholy splendour.

"It seems to me just as imbecile, just as infernal, to have to go to the office on Monday," said Jonathan, "as it always has done and always will do. To spend all the best years of one's life sitting on a stool from nine to five, scratching in somebody's ledger! It's a queer use to make of one's . . . one and only life, isn't it? Or do I fondly dream?" He rolled over on the grass and looked up at Linda. "Tell me, what is the difference between my life and that of an ordinary prisoner. The only difference I can see is that I put myself in jail and nobody's ever going to let me out. That's a more intolerable situation than the other. For if I'd been — pushed in, against my will — kicking, even — once the door was locked, or at any rate in five years or so, I might have accepted the fact and begun to take an interest in the flight of flies or counting the warder's steps along the passage with particular attention to variations of tread and so on. But as it is, I'm like an insect that's flown into a room of its own accord. I dash against the walls, dash against the windows, flop against the ceiling, do everything on God's earth, in fact, except fly out again. And all the while I'm thinking, like that moth, or that butterfly, or whatever it is, "The shortness of life! The shortness of life!" I've only one night or one day, and there's this vast dangerous garden, waiting out there, undiscovered, unexplored."

"But, if you feel like that, why—" began Linda quickly.

"*Ah*!" cried Jonathan. And that "Ah!" was somehow almost exultant. "There you have me. Why? Why indeed? There's the maddening, mysterious question. Why don't I fly out again? There's the window or the door or whatever it was I came in by. It's not hopelessly shut — is it? Why don't I find it and be off? Answer me that, little sister." But he gave her no time to answer.

"I'm exactly like that insect again. For some reason" — Jonathan paused between the words — "it's

not allowed, it's forbidden, it's against the insect law, to stop banging and flopping and crawling up the pane even for an instant. Why don't I leave the office? Why don't I seriously consider, this moment, for instance, what it is that prevents me leaving? It's not as though I'm tremendously tied. I've two boys to provide for, but, after all, they're boys. I could cut off to sea, or get a job up-country, or—" Suddenly he smiled at Linda and said in a changed voice, as if he were confiding a secret, "Weak . . . weak. No stamina. No anchor. No guiding principle, let us call it." But then the dark velvety voice rolled out:

Would ye hear the story
How it unfolds itself . . .
and they were silent.

The sun had set. In the western sky there were great masses of crushed-up rose-coloured clouds. Broad beams of light shone through the clouds and beyond them as if they would cover the whole sky. Overhead the blue faded; it turned a pale gold, and the bush outlined against it gleamed dark and brilliant like metal. Sometimes when those beams of light show in the sky they are very awful. They remind you that up there sits Jehovah, the jealous God, the Almighty, Whose eye is upon you, ever watchful, never weary. You remember that at His coming the whole earth will shake into one ruined graveyard; the cold, bright angels will drive you this way and that, and there will be no time to explain what could be explained so simply. . . . But to-night it seemed to Linda there was something infinitely joyful and loving in those silver beams. And now no sound came from the sea. It breathed softly as if it would draw that tender, joyful beauty into its own bosom.

"It's all wrong, it's all wrong," came the shadowy voice of Jonathan. "It's not the scene, it's not the setting for . . . three stools, three desks, three inkpots and a wire blind."

Linda knew that he would never change, but she said, "Is it too late, even now?"

"I'm old — I'm old," intoned Jonathan. He bent towards her, he passed his hand over his head. "Look!" His black hair was speckled all over with silver, like the breast plumage of a black fowl.

Linda was surprised. She had no idea that he was grey. And yet, as he stood up beside her and sighed and stretched, she saw him, for the first time, not resolute, not gallant, not careless, but touched already with age. He looked very tall on the darkening grass, and the thought crossed her mind, "He is like a weed."

Jonathan stooped again and kissed her fingers.

"Heaven reward thy sweet patience, lady mine," he murmured. "I must go seek those heirs to my fame and fortune. . . ." He was gone.

XI /

Light shone in the windows of the bungalow. Two square patches of gold fell upon the pinks and the peaked marigolds. Florrie, the cat, came out on to the verandah and sat on the top step, her white paws close together, her tail curled round. She looked content, as though she had been waiting for this moment all day.

"Thank goodness, it's getting late," said Florrie. "Thank goodness, the long day is over." Her greengage eyes opened.

Presently there sounded the rumble of the coach, the cracking of Kelly's whip. It came near enough for one to hear the voices of the men from town, talking loudly together. It stopped at the Burnells' gate.

Stanley was half-way up the path before he saw Linda. "Is that you, darling?"

"Yes, Stanley."

He leapt across the flower-bed and seized her in his arms. She was enfolded in that familiar, eager, strong embrace.

"Forgive me, darling, forgive me,"

stammered Stanley, and he put his hand under her chin and lifted her face to him.

"Forgive you?" smiled Linda. "But whatever for?"

"Good God! You can't have forgotten," cried Stanley Burnell. "I've thought of nothing else all day. I've had the hell of a day. I made up my mind to dash out and telegraph, and then I thought the wire mightn't reach you before I did. I've been in tortures, Linda."

"But, Stanley," said Linda, "what must I forgive you for?"

"Linda!" — Stanley was very hurt — "didn't you realise — you must have realised — I went away without saying good-bye to you this morning? I can't imagine how I can have done such a thing. My confounded temper, of course. But — well" — and he sighed and took her in his arms again — "I've suffered for it enough today."

"What's that you've got in your hand?" asked Linda. "New gloves? Let me see."

"Oh, just a cheap pair of wash-leather ones," said Stanley humbly. "I noticed Bell was wearing some in the coach this morning, so, as I was passing the shop, I dashed in and got myself a pair. What are you smiling at? You don't think it was wrong of me, do you?"

"On the *con*-trary, darling," said Linda, "I think it was most sensible."

She pulled one of the large, pale gloves on her own fingers and looked at her hand, turning it this way and that. She was still smiling.

Stanley wanted to say, "I was thinking of you the whole time I bought them." It was true, but for some reason he couldn't say it. "Let's go in," said he.

XII /

Why does one feel so different at night? Why is it so exciting to be awake when everybody else is asleep? Late — it is very late! And yet every moment you feel more and more wakeful, as though you were slowly, almost with every breath, waking up into a new, wonderful, far more thrilling and exciting world than the daylight one. And what is this queer sensation that you're a conspirator? Lightly, stealthily you move about your room. You take something off the dressing-table and put it down again without a sound. And everything, even the bedpost, knows you, responds, shares your secret. . . .

You're not very fond of your room by day. You never think about it. You're in and out, the door opens and slams, the cupboard creaks. You sit down on the side of your bed, change your shoes and dash out again. A dive down to the glass, two pins in your hair, powder your nose and off again. But now — it's suddenly dear to you. It's a darling little funny room. It's yours. Oh, what a joy it is to own things! Mine — my own!

"My very own for ever?"

"Yes." Their lips met.

No, of course, that had nothing to do with it. That was all nonsense and rubbish. But, in spite of herself, Beryl saw so plainly two people standing in the middle of her room. Her arms were round his neck; he held her. And now he whispered, "My beauty, my little beauty!" She jumped off her bed, ran over to the window and kneeled on the window-seat, with her elbows on the sill. But the beautiful night, the garden, every bush, every leaf, even the white palings, even the stars, were conspirators too. So bright was the moon that the flowers were bright as by day; the shadow of the nasturtiums, exquisite lily-like leaves and wide-open flowers, lay across the silvery verandah. The manuka tree, bent by the southerly winds, was like a bird on one leg stretching out a wing.

But when Beryl looked at the bush, it seemed to her the bush was sad.

"We are dumb trees, reaching up in the night, imploring we know not what," said the sorrowful bush.

It is true when you are by yourself and you think about life, it is always sad. All that excitement and so on has a way of suddenly leaving you, and it's as though, in the silence, somebody called your name, and you heard your name for the first time. "Beryl!"

"Yes, I'm here. I'm Beryl. Who wants me?"

"Beryl!"

"Let me come."

It is lonely living by oneself. Of course, there are relations, friends, heaps of them; but that's not what she means. She wants someone who will find the Beryl they none of them know, who will expect her to be that Beryl always. She wants a lover.

"Take me away from all these other people, my love. Let us go far away. Let us live our life, all new, all ours, from the very beginning. Let us make our fire. Let us sit down to eat together. Let us have long talks at night."

And the thought was almost, "Save me, my love. Save me!"

. . . "Oh, go on! Don't be a prude, my dear. You enjoy yourself while you're young. That's my advice." And a high rush of silly laughter joined Mrs Harry Kember's loud, indifferent neigh.

You see, it's so frightfully difficult when you've nobody. You're so at the mercy of things. You can't just be rude. And you've always this horror of seeming inexperienced and stuffy like the other ninnies at the Bay. And — and it's fascinating to know you've power over people. Yes, that is fascinating. . . . Oh why, oh why doesn't "he" come soon?

If I go on living here, thought Beryl, anything may happen to me.

"But how do you know he is coming at all?" mocked a small voice within her.

But Beryl dismissed it. She couldn't be left. Other people, perhaps, but not she. It wasn't possible to think that Beryl Fairfield never married, that lovely, fascinating girl.

"Do you remember Beryl Fairfield?"

"Remember her! As if I could forget her! It was one summer at the Bay that I saw her. She was standing on the beach in a blue" — no, pink — "muslin frock, holding on a big cream" — no, black — "straw hat. But it's years ago now."

"She's as lovely as ever, more so if anything."

Beryl smiled, bit her lip, and gazed over the garden. As she gazed, she saw somebody, a man, leave the road, step along the paddock beside their palings as if he was coming straight towards her. Her heart beat. Who was it? Who could it be? It couldn't be a burglar, certainly not a burglar, for he was smoking and he strolled lightly. Beryl's heart leapt; it seemed to turn right over and then to stop. She recognised him.

"Good evening, Miss Beryl," said the voice softly.

"Good evening."

"Won't you come for a little walk?" it drawled.

Come for a walk — at that time of night! "I couldn't. Everybody's in bed. Everybody's asleep."

"Oh," said the voice lightly, and a whiff of sweet smoke reached her. "What does everybody matter? Do come! It's such a fine night. There's not a soul about."

Beryl shook her head. But already something stirred in her, something reared its head.

The voice said, "Frightened?" It mocked, "Poor little girl!"

"Not in the least," said she. As she spoke that weak thing within her seemed to uncoil, to grow suddenly tremendously strong; she longed to go!

And just as if this was quite understood by the other, the voice said, gently and softly, but finally, "Come along!"

Beryl stepped over her low window; crossed the verandah, ran down the grass to the gate. He was there before her.

"That's right," breathed the voice, and it teased, "You're not frightened, are you? You're not frightened?"

She was; now she was here she was terrified and it seemed to her everything was different. The moonlight stared and glittered; the shadows were like bars of iron. Her hand was taken.

"Not in the least," she said lightly. "Why should I be?"

Her hand was pulled gently, tugged. She held back.

"No, I'm not coming any further," said Beryl.

"Oh, rot!" Harry Kember didn't believe her. "Come along! We'll just go as far as that fuchsia bush. Come along!"

The fuchsia bush was tall. It fell over the fence in a shower. There was a little pit of darkness beneath.

"No, really, I don't want to," said Beryl.

For a moment Harry Kember didn't answer. Then he came close to her, turned to her, smiled and said quickly, "Don't be silly! Don't be silly!"

His smile was something she'd never seen before. Was he drunk? That bright, blind, terrifying smile froze her with horror. What was she doing? How had she got here? The stern garden asked her as the gate pushed open, and quick as a cat Harry Kember came through and snatched her to him.

"Cold little devil! Cold little devil!" said the hateful voice.

But Beryl was strong. She slipped, ducked, wrenched free. "You are vile, vile," said she.

"Then why in God's name did you come?" stammered Harry Kember.

Nobody answered him.

A cloud, small, serene, floated across the moon. In that moment of darkness the sea sounded deep, troubled. Then the cloud sailed away, and the sound of the sea was a vague murmur, as though it waked out of a dark dream. All was still.

OUR HEROES

In a land where shouting one's own praises is a no-no and 'tall poppies' are mown down in an instant, New Zealanders like their heroes to have their feet on the ground — even if they are 30,000 feet up a mountain.

SIR EDMUND HILLARY

/1919–2008

One of the most dearly loved New Zealanders of all time, this shy beekeeper from Tuakau, a country town near Auckland, brought his country to world prominence just days before the coronation of Queen Elizabeth II. Hillary, with Sherpa Tenzing Norgay, was the first to reach the summit of the world's highest mountain, Mt Everest, on 29 May 1953. Not only did we love the fact of his achievement, but we also loved the style with which he completed it — encapsulated by his famous words to fellow climber George Lowe on return to camp: 'Well, George, we knocked the bastard off.'

As well as further adventuring in the South Pole and the Himalayas, Hillary subsequently turned his fame into a force for good, setting up a trust to support Sherpa communities in Nepal and other humanitarian work. He remained humble and accessible, with his home phone number listed in the telephone directory. 'In some ways I believe I epitomise the average New Zealander,' Hillary once wrote. 'I have modest abilities, I combine these with a good deal of determination, and I rather like to succeed.'

KATE SHEPPARD

/1847–1934

Modern New Zealand women take their right to vote for granted, but if it hadn't been for the actions of pioneering suffragette Kate Sheppard it might have been a different story. Sheppard emigrated to New Zealand with her widowed mother in 1869 and became involved with the fledgling New Zealand Women's Christian Temperance Union, agitating for franchise reform. She helped organise petitions calling for votes for women; these were signed by more than 60,000 New Zealand women before legislation was reluctantly passed through Parliament in 1893, in time for that year's general election — making New Zealand the first country in the world to confer universal franchise on women. (Kate's home country did not allow all women to vote until 1928.) Although teetotaller Kate might not have approved, we should still raise a glass to her achievements each polling day.

ERNEST, BARON RUTHERFORD OF NELSON

/1871–1937

Pioneering scientist Ernest Rutherford's parents might not have been able to spell very well — his name was registered incorrectly as Earnest — but they instilled in him a love of education and a desire to succeed beyond the usual expectations of a country boy. Born near Nelson in 1871, Rutherford excelled at school, where he won several scholarships, and he earned three university degrees before he turned 23. He then took his analytical mind to England, where he did important research at Cambridge University, before making his most significant discovery while working at the Victoria University of Manchester. Rutherford's investigations in 1911 resulted in the modern nuclear model of the atom, while in 1917 he went further and 'split the atom', converting nitrogen atoms into oxygen. Rutherford died in 1937 and is buried in Westminster Abbey. His most famous quote is still entirely relevant in the New Zealand of the early twenty-first century: 'We haven't got the money, so we've got to think.'

JACK
LOVELOCK

/1910–49

In 1936, at the Berlin Olympics, Jack Lovelock crossed the finish line first to win gold in the 1500 metres. Millions of people worldwide listened eagerly over the wireless airwaves as the BBC commentator abandoned his British reserve to shout 'My God, he's done it! Jack! Come on!' Lovelock's grace under pressure and perfectly timed burst of speed over the last 300 metres became legendary, as he set a new world record of 3 minutes 47.8 seconds to win New Zealand's first ever Olympic gold medal in athletics.

BURT MUNRO

/1899–1978

Backyard mechanic and genius innovator Burt Munro was born in Edendale, Southland, in 1899. When he was 21 he bought the Indian Scout motorcycle that would shape the quest of his life. From 1948 until his record-breaking runs at Bonneville Salt Flats in Utah in the 1960s, he worked full-time on getting that Indian to go faster and faster, using his Kiwi ingenuity to make or alter parts and fittings. He set his first speed record at Bonneville at the age of 62, and his 1967 speed of 183.586 mph (295.453 kph) for the Flying One Mile on a 1000cc bike still stands today.

BRUCE MCLAREN

/1937–70

The famous Formula One team McLaren was established in 1963 by a talented young driver from Auckland, whose death on the test racetrack at the age of just 33, in 1970, cut short a glittering career. As a child McLaren suffered from Perthes disease, a hip-joint deterioration problem, but he cast aside his walking frame at age 14 to take up motor racing, first in an Austin 7 Ulster and then in Europe. In 1959, aged 22, McLaren became the youngest driver ever to win a World Championship F1 race. In 1966 he set up McLaren Racing Ltd, letting others drive while he concentrated on design, building and development. Four years later he died on the test track, but many famous drivers, including Jensen Button and Lewis Hamilton, have continued to race in his name.

SIR PETER BLAKE

/1948–2001

Sir Peter Blake combined typical Kiwi humility and practicality with a steely nerve and a determination to succeed. Born in Auckland, Blake began sailing at the age of five. By 25 he was sailing around the world, taking part in the inaugural Whitbread Round the World race in 1973–74. By the 1980s he was running his own campaigns, first on *Ceramco New Zealand* and then *Lion New Zealand*, before blitzing the event in unprecedented style aboard the yacht nicknamed 'Big Red', *Steinlager 2*, in 1989–90. Blake then took on the America's Cup, leading Team New Zealand to victory in 1995 and 2000, before turning his focus to environmental advocacy. Tragically, while on a conservation-focused trip to the Amazon in late 2001 he was shot and killed by pirates. Blake's most famous quip is also quintessentially Kiwi: 'If it was easy, everyone would be doing it.'

SIR RAY AVERY

/1947–

Ray Avery was born in poverty in England, but his life turned a corner when he emigrated to New Zealand in the 1970s. Avery made his name and fortune in pharmaceuticals, and in 2003 established global aid agency Medicine Mondiale, a network of scientific, medical and business experts who donate their knowledge and time to develop medical solutions for the Third World. Avery worked with the Fred Hollows Foundation to develop cost-effective production of lenses for cataract surgery in Eritrea and Nepal, and continues to work on affordable healthcare solutions for developing countries, such as a portable baby incubator, improved infant formulas, and an intravenous fluid controller. Avery was appointed Knight Grand Companion of the New Zealand Order of Merit in 2011 for services to philanthropy.

OUR
POETS

W e must ask from time to time, who are we? Where have we been and what shall we become? How does this land speak to us?

Three great poems tell that story, place us in this land, and express our relationship with it.

LANDFALL IN UNKNOWN SEAS

*The 300th Anniversary of the Discovery of New Zealand
by Abel Tasman, 13 December, 1642*

ALLEN CURNOW

I /

Simply by sailing in a new direction
You could enlarge the world.
You picked your captain,
Keen on discoveries, tough enough to make them,
Whatever vessels could be spared from other
More urgent service for a year's adventure;
Took stock of the more probable conjectures
About the Unknown to be traversed, all
Guesses at golden coasts and tales of monsters
To be digested into plain instructions
For likely and unlikely situations.

All this resolved and done, you launched the whole
On a fine morning, the best time of year,
Skies widening and the oceanic furies
Subdued by summer illumination; time
To go and to be gazed at going
On a fine morning, in the Name of God
Into the nameless waters of the world.

O you had estimated all the chances
Of business in those waters, the world's waters
Yet unexploited.
                              But more than the sea-empire's
Cannon, the dogs of bronze and iron barking
From Timor to the Straits, backed up the challenge.
Between you and the South an orderly enmity
Lodged in the searching mind that would not tolerate
So huge a hegemony of ignorance.
There, where your Indies had already sprinkled
Their tribes like ocean rains, you aimed your voyage;
Like them invoked your God, gave seas to history
And islands to new hazardous tomorrows.

II /

Suddenly exhilaration
Went off like a gun, the whole
Horizon, the long chase done,
Hove to. There was the seascape
Crammed with coast, surprising
As new lands will, the sailor
Moving on the face of the waters,
Watching the earth take shape
Round the unearthly summits, brighter
Than its emerging colour.

Yet this, no far fool's errand,
Was less than the heart desired,
In its old Indian dream
The glittering gulfs ascending
Past palaces and mountains
Making one architecture.

Here the uplifted structure,
Peak and pillar of cloud —
O splendour of desolation — reared
Tall from the pit of the swell,
With a shadow, a finger of wind, forbade
Hopes of a lucky landing.

Always to islanders danger
Is what comes over the sea;
Over the yellow sands and the clear
Shallows, the dull filament
Flickers, the blood of strangers:
Dear discovered the Sailor
O in a flash, in a flat calm,
A clash of boats in the bay
And the day marred with murder.
The dead required no further
Warning to keep their distance;
The rest, noting the future,
Pushed on with a reconnaissance
To the north; and sailed away.

III /

Well, home is the Sailor, and that is a chapter
In a schoolbook, a relevant yesterday
We thought we knew all about, being much apter
     To profit, sure of our ground,
No murderers mooring in our Golden Bay.

But now there are no more islands to be found
And the eye scans risky horizons of its own
In unsettled weather, and murmurs of drowned
     Haunt their familiar beaches —
Who navigates us toward what unknown

But not improbable provinces? Who reaches
A future down for us from the high shelf
Of spiritual daring? Not those speeches
     Pinning on the Past like a decoration
For merit that congratulates itself,
O not the self-important celebration
Or most painstaking history, can release
The current of a discoverer's elation
     And silence the voices saying,
'Here is the world's end where wonders cease'.

Only by a more faithful memory, laying
On him the half-light of a diffident glory,
The Sailor lives, and stands beside us, paying
     Out into our time's wave
The stain of blood that writes an island story.

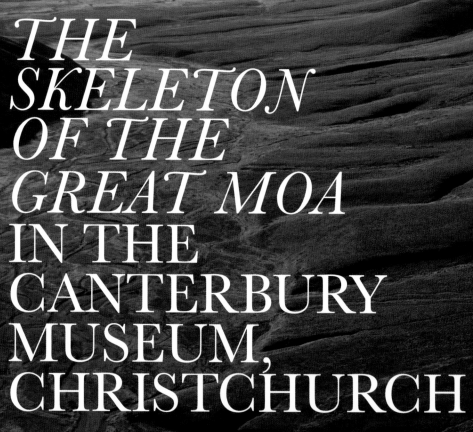

THE SKELETON OF THE GREAT MOA IN THE CANTERBURY MUSEUM, CHRISTCHURCH

ALLEN CURNOW

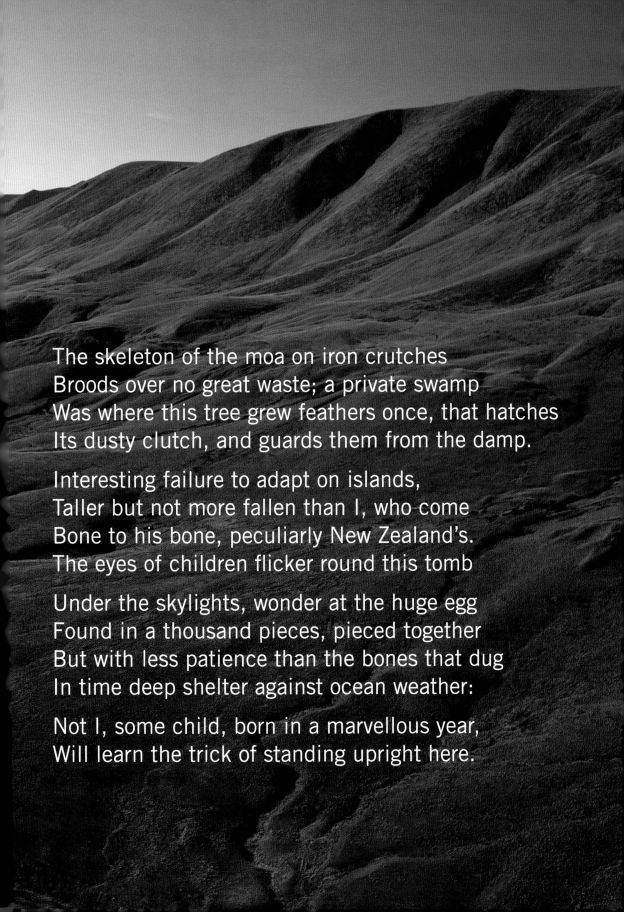

The skeleton of the moa on iron crutches
Broods over no great waste; a private swamp
Was where this tree grew feathers once, that hatches
Its dusty clutch, and guards them from the damp.

Interesting failure to adapt on islands,
Taller but not more fallen than I, who come
Bone to his bone, peculiarly New Zealand's.
The eyes of children flicker round this tomb

Under the skylights, wonder at the huge egg
Found in a thousand pieces, pieced together
But with less patience than the bones that dug
In time deep shelter against ocean weather:

Not I, some child, born in a marvellous year,
Will learn the trick of standing upright here.

ELEGY IN THE CLUTHA VALLEY

(In memory of Denis Glover)

BRIAN TURNER

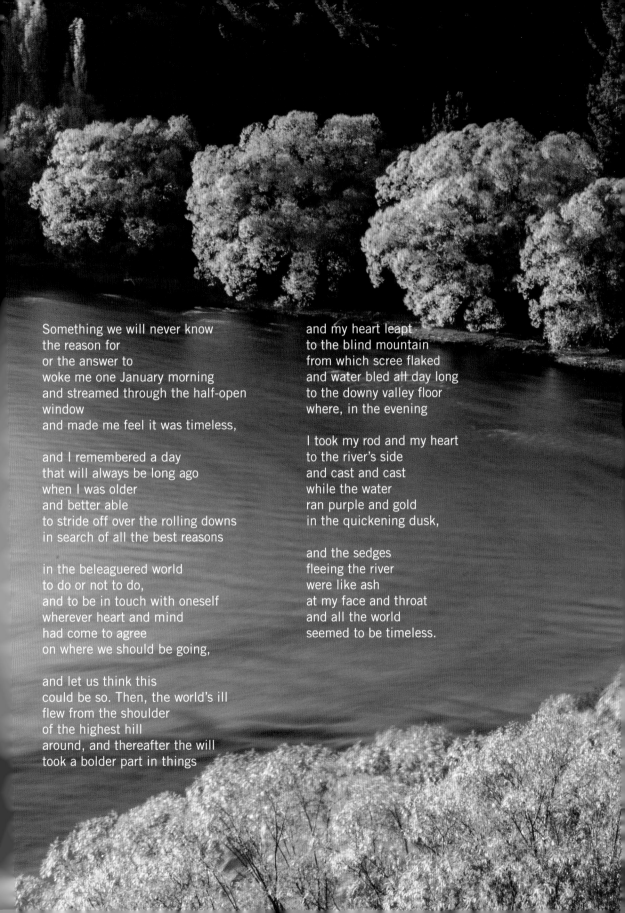

Something we will never know
the reason for
or the answer to
woke me one January morning
and streamed through the half-open
window
and made me feel it was timeless,

and I remembered a day
that will always be long ago
when I was older
and better able
to stride off over the rolling downs
in search of all the best reasons

in the beleaguered world
to do or not to do,
and to be in touch with oneself
wherever heart and mind
had come to agree
on where we should be going,

and let us think this
could be so. Then, the world's ill
flew from the shoulder
of the highest hill
around, and thereafter the will
took a bolder part in things

and my heart leapt
to the blind mountain
from which scree flaked
and water bled all day long
to the downy valley floor
where, in the evening

I took my rod and my heart
to the river's side
and cast and cast
while the water
ran purple and gold
in the quickening dusk,

and the sedges
fleeing the river
were like ash
at my face and throat
and all the world
seemed to be timeless.

THE THINGS WE DO FOR FUN

WE LIKE TO DRIVE JETBOATS AT HIGH SPEED AT CANYON WALLS

Farmer Charles Hamilton, better known as Bill, was a self-taught engineer who had dabbled in motor racing and building excavators when he came up with the idea for a jet-propelled boat that could traverse shallow rivers, such as those of his native Canterbury, at high speeds. Research and development on the family farm and the rivers of the Mackenzie Country led to the Hamilton jet, now exported and in use worldwide for both thrillseeking and practical purposes, opening up previously unnavigable rivers.

WE LIKE TO HEAD FOR THE HILLS

We are day walkers, overnight trampers, climbers, expeditionists. The tracks we love follow Māori trading paths from Canterbury across the Alps to the West Coast for pounamu (greenstone), for example, or trails that the early European explorers and surveyors blazed up river valleys and through endless thickets of spiky matagouri, or tracks hacked into the land as bushmen cleared our northern hills and offshore islands of the mighty kauri.

There are thousands of kilometres of paths leading us to great forests, glaciers, river terraces, tussock-lands, escarpments, volcanic craters, waterfalls, rock faces, fragile wetlands, tarns, hot pools, and much more. One mighty track, Te Araroa: The Long Pathway, takes us right through the country from the top of the North Island to the bottom of the South.

There are huts out there in our wild places. Some are venerable, spider-webbed, their interiors smudged with the soot of decades of cooking fires and Tilley lamps burning at night to light card games and routes traced on maps. Some are newer, built to withstand howling gales and mighty dumps of snow.

We can roam free . . . and we are blessed.

WE LIKE
TO JUMP
OFF BRIDGES
WITH RUBBER
BANDS TIED
TO OUR
ANKLES

Why did it take a New Zealander to think of the idea of jumping off high things for fun, secured only by a large rubber band around the ankles? Was no one else crazy enough? In fact, the practice of what became bungy jumping began with the Pentecost Islanders of Vanuatu, who leap from timber towers with vines tied to their ankles, wearing only a penis sheath. In the 1980s, bungy pioneers AJ Hackett and Henry van Asch, inspired by footage of imitation jumps staged by Oxford University's Dangerous Sports Club in the 1970s, brought the practice to a wider audience. After developing a latex bungy cord with Auckland University scientists, and experimenting on themselves and their friends, Hackett went public with a daring stunt off the Eiffel Tower in Paris in June 1987. The first commercial operation was set up at Queenstown's Kawarau Bridge the following year, heralding the birth of New Zealand's adventure tourism industry.

WE LIKE TO PLAY RUGBY

Rugby union remains the country's national game, and we celebrate and mourn along with the successes and stumbles of the All Blacks. On winter Saturdays throughout the country, rugby fields churn with mud, steam with rucks, and resound with the cheers of spectators and sideline experts.

New Zealand's first organised game of rugby union was played in Nelson in 1870; today nearly 200,000 New Zealanders take part. New Zealand's first nationally selected team toured Australia in 1884, but the name All Blacks didn't gain traction until 1905–06, when a national side now known as 'the Originals' toured England and Wales. It is still debated whether the name came from their black uniforms or whether they played as if they were 'all backs'.

WE LIKE TO CELEBRATE

We're a country of festivals. Our music festivals are legendary, and ever since the famous Nambassa, which got going in the the Coromandel hills in the 1970s, events like Rhythm and Vines, Camp A Lo Hum, Splore and Big Day Out form a rite of passage.

We love to celebrate Matariki, Diwali, Pasifika, our Celtic forebears with Highland Games, Chinese New Year, the arts, film, opera, fireworks, snow and so much more.

WE LIKE TO PLAY CRICKET

A bit of leisurely running, a lot of standing about, breaks for tea, shouts of 'Well caught!' . . . This most English of games has been popular in New Zealand since the first settlers cleared enough bush to whack a ball around. The missionary Henry Williams recorded a game being played at the mission station in Paihia, in the Bay of Islands, in 1832. The equipment required is minimal — a bat, a ball, and some sticks for stumps — and no Kiwi summer is complete without a few games of backyard or beach cricket.

WE LIKE TO PLAY NETBALL

Every winter Saturday, rain or shine, throughout the land hundreds of girls and women in short skirts and lettered bibs leap about netball courts. Known as women's basketball until the 1970s, netball involves teams of seven players on an indoor or outdoor court. One of the few sports played almost exclusively by women, netball has a huge following in New Zealand from school level upwards, and is the sport with the largest participation in the country at secondary school level.

New Zealand teams compete in a trans-Tasman professional franchise competition, and the national side, the Silver Ferns, has won the world championships three times and gold medals at two Commonwealth Games.

Wing Defence, Goal Attack — on the netball court New Zealand women are Amazons with a round ball.

WE LIKE MESSING ABOUT IN BOATS

The first European settlers in New Zealand were quick to set up regattas and sailing races — Auckland's annual Anniversary Day Regatta in late January was first held in 1840 — and working craft such as the mullet boats which brought home fish to the markets were fine-tuned for recreational racing. New Zealand sailors Peter Mander and Jack Cropp won the country's first Olympic sailing gold medal in 1956 — and it was the first time a Kiwi yachting team had been sent to the Olympics!

Our first major international success in bigger boats came in 1969, when Chris Bouzaid and his team took the One Ton Cup off the coast of Germany. In the 1980s and 1990s New Zealand became dominant in offshore sailing, winning events such as the Whitbread Round the World race; then, in 1995, a New Zealand team brought home sailing's most high-profile trophy, the America's Cup. Kiwi sailors are now ubiquitous at regattas and on racing teams around the world, and our boatbuilders, riggers, and sail- and spar-makers outfit the world's racing boats and superyachts.

WE LIKE TO CAMP

Our country is littered with places to pitch a tent, be it in splendidly isolated back-to-basics campgrounds run by the Department of Conservation or holiday parks with evening entertainment, swimming pools, fancy kitchens and modern shower blocks.

We love that when we are camping it can take all day to do the simplest things: hand-wash our clothes and peg them to the guy ropes of the tent, cook up rice on the Coleman stove, blow up the air bed by hand because we forgot to bring the pump . . .

We love that we camp close to total strangers, who within half an hour are friendly neighbours and are lending us their tomato sauce because we forgot to pack that, too.

We love the shower blocks that run on a continual feed of 20 cent coins, the fridges that are stuffed with someone's day's-worth of fishing, nicely filleted . . . and that they might just offer us some to toss in the pan.

We love the democracy of it. When it pours with rain all night *everyone* is out with spades digging trenches around the base of their tents, whether they arrived in a Range Rover or a battered old ute. Everyone gets bitten by sandflies. Everyone is battered by days of wind. We are all one under our canvas awnings.

WE LIKE TO GET ICE CREAMS FROM THE DAIRY ON A HOT DAY

In you go, your hair matted with salt from the day's swimming, the grains of sand stuck to your jandals flicking onto the lino; the floor of the diary is gritty with it. There's a queue. Someone's just ordered six cones, and they want a mix of scoop flavours in each. *Sigh*.

You shuffle to the front. One scoop or two? Hokey pokey or raspberry ripple? Outside in the sun, the ice cream is running down the side of the cone within minutes. You need to lick it more quickly, but then it'll be finished that much sooner. Soggy cone-tip, or crisp and crunchy to the last bite? It's *that* personal.

WE LIKE TO PLAY IN THE SNOW

In the South Island we ski in the Southern Alps, in the North we ski on volcanoes. New Zealand's ski industry started in the 1930s in a homespun way, with intrepid individuals making their own skis and building simple ski-club huts on slopes in remote places.

By the 1940s, some of the slog of getting back up to the top of the slopes had been taken out with the installation of utilitarian rope-tows, but it wasn't until serious money went into the big commercial field at Coronet Peak near Queenstown that anything as glamorous as a chairlift seemed possible.

Mount Cook Airlines flew skiers to the snow, and eventually new fields such as Treble Cone, Cardrona and the Remarkables opened up. Heliskiing, snowboarding, snowmaking and night skiing, in both northern and southern fields, seem a long way away from the early, pioneering years of basic rudimentary equipment and heavy woollen clothing. But our love of fun in the snow endures.

WE LIKE TO STAY IN TINY LITTLE COTTAGES

The bach, the crib . . . modest places, knocked up over a few weekends by a bunch of mates, made of fibrolite and recycled windows and whatever else was at hand. A long-drop loo out the back. In more salubrious residences, perhaps an indoor bathroom. Electricity? Often not.

Bunkbeds with lumpy mattresses, old magazines, well-used board games, tide charts taped to the wall, shells from beach collections piled in a midden on a shelf, a dinghy and a rusting lawnmower round the back, the smell of must and dust when the door is opened after a long gap between visits.

The sun pouring in, swimsuits and towels drying on the clothesline, barbecues and salads, the bach owners next door over for a beer at sundown . . . Summer, long weekends, resourceful yet easy living . . . These are the little coastal and mountain places that are lodged within our DNA.

WE LIKE TO PUSH OURSELVES TO THE LIMIT

We could be slightly mad. Evidence? Every year for 32 years, 8000 of us have run up the sand of Kumara Beach on the South Island's west coast, through the Southern Alps via mountain passes and creek valleys, avoiding jagged rocks, tussock and spinifex as we go, then leapt into kayaks and paddled down the mighty Waimakariri River, cycled across the Canterbury Plains, paddled through Christchurch and finally hurled ourselves at the finish line on Sumner Beach on the South Island's east coast. Amazingly, the fastest people have done this 243-kilometre race in a scorching 10 hours and 40 minutes in just one day.

But that's not all. We run and bike from Lake Wanaka to Arrowtown across the Crown Range mountains on the Motutapu Challenge. We race our bikes 160 kilometres around Lake Taupō. We run marathons and half-marathons. We swim across harbours and lakes and along coasts. We adventure-race for days at a stretch on the Coromandel, or across the Southern Alps. We are driven.

WE LIKE
TO GO
DOWN TO
THE SEA

We have over 15,000 kilometres of coastlline. For
some of its length that coast is benign, fringed with
white sand and the dipping boughs of pōhutukawa.
In others it's wild, roaring, challenging, wind-
buffeted, tough. But whatever its tenor, we are all
drawn to wandering there. We swim, we run, we
ride horses, we fish, we sail, we surf. And when we
look to the horizon we are acutely aware of how far
we are from any other land. Rather than terrifying
us, that distance sets us free.

WE LIKE TO DRINK COFFEE

With the exception of a handful of bohemian cafés run by European emigrés in Auckland and Wellington, and the venerable coffee roasters Stewart's in Dunedin, we were a land of tea drinkers until the 1980s. Most of us had never seen an espresso machine. And when we did drink coffee, it was instant.

It all changed in the mid-1980s. Enterprising and visionary coffee roasters imported roasting machines and set up shop: Millers in Auckland, followed by Atomic; Havana and Caffe L'affare in Wellington.

Cafés sprang up everywhere and started serving short blacks (espressos) and that New Zealand invention, the flat white, to patrons who suddenly saw that all along there had been something missing from the country's cultural life: café society. And so it was that New Zealand bucked the trend when the Starbucks empire landed in the late 1990s. It found New Zealanders largely indifferent to its products: we had our own way of making, serving and drinking coffee, thanks very much.

Now you can get a great coffee almost anywhere, boutique roasteries are legion, and coffee outfits such as Allpress are making flat whites in London, Tokyo and Sydney. We're tea drinkers no more.

WE LOVE TO ENTERTAIN AT HOME

SO FEEL
FREE TO
DROP
IN FOR
*A NICE
CUP OF
TEA AND
A BITE
TO EAT*

GINGERBREAD

We like to hand recipes on! This recipe is from Pipi Café in Havelock North, and they got it from the Waihi School cookbook, *Fuel for Your Family*.

Makes 1 large or 2 small loaves

2 CUPS FLOUR
1 CUP SOFT BROWN SUGAR
1 TSP BAKING POWDER
1 TSP BAKING SODA
2 DSSP GROUND GINGER
½ TSP MIXED SPICE
½ TSP GROUND NUTMEG
1 TSP GROUND CINNAMON
250 G BUTTER
1 CUP GOLDEN SYRUP
3 EGGS, LIGHTLY BEATEN
1 CUP MILK
ICING SUGAR FOR DUSTING

Preheat the oven to 160°C. Grease two loaf tins and line with greaseproof paper.

Sift the dry ingredients into a large bowl.

Melt the butter and golden syrup together.

Add the eggs to the dry mixture, followed by the butter and golden syrup, and the milk. Mix together and pour the batter into the loaf tins.

Put in the oven and cook for 50–60 minutes, or until a knife poked in the centre comes out clean.

Cool in the tins for 10 minutes, then turn out onto a wire rack. Dust with icing sugar before serving. It will keep for 3–4 days.

CHEESY SCONES

All you need for basic scones is flour and baking powder, salt, milk and a little butter. Best eaten warm from the oven. This recipe is from New Zealand baking legend Jo Seagar.

Makes 10–12

3 CUPS SELF-RAISING FLOUR
½ TSP SALT
1 CUP GRATED TASTY CHEESE (AGED CHEDDAR)
1 CUP MILK
25 G BUTTER
EXTRA MILK FOR BRUSHING
EXTRA GRATED CHEESE

Preheat the oven to 200°C. Coat an oven tray with non-stick baking spray.

Place the flour, salt and cheese in a large bowl. Heat the milk and butter together in the microwave, or in a small saucepan, until the butter has melted. Pour the wet ingredients into the dry ingredients and mix to form a soft, moist dough. A little extra cold milk may be required to get the dough to the right consistency.

Dust the bench with flour and tip out the dough. Press out to a thickness of 3 cm and cut out the scones, either in squares or with a round cookie cutter, and place on the prepared tray. I like soft-sided scones, so I place mine close together so they touch when they rise in the oven.

Brush the tops with milk, add a sprinkling of grated cheese and bake for 12–15 minutes until golden brown and cooked through. Cool on a wire rack, covering with a clean tea towel to keep them soft and moist.

Serve warm with butter. These scones keep well and can be reheated in a microwave to freshen them up.

ANZAC BISCUITS

This recipe is from well-known New Zealand baker Dean Brettschneider. Chewy, oaty biscuits were sent to soldiers on the front line, including at Gallipoli, during the First World War because they kept well and were good for dunking in tea. Most recipes for Anzac biscuits do not include eggs, which were in short supply during wartime. Dean makes his a little bit fancier than the norm with the addition of dried fruit.

Makes 18

140 G BUTTER

60 G GOLDEN SYRUP

80 G ROLLED OATS

70 G SUNFLOWER SEEDS, LIGHTLY TOASTED

50 G SULTANAS

60 G DRIED FIGS, STEMS DISCARDED, CUT INTO 8–10 PIECES

75 G CHOPPED DRIED APRICOTS

65 G LONG-THREAD COCONUT (SUBSTITUTE ORDINARY DESICCATED COCONUT IF NECESSARY)

125 G STANDARD (PLAIN) FLOUR

90 G BROWN SUGAR

5 G BAKING SODA

2 TBSP BOILING WATER

Preheat the oven to 180°C. Line a baking tray with baking paper.

Melt the butter and golden syrup together in a saucepan.

Place all the remaining ingredients except the baking soda and the water in a large mixing bowl. Stir to combine.

Place the baking soda in a jug and pour the boiling water over it, stirring well to dissolve. Add to the butter and golden syrup mixture, then pour the wet ingredients into the dry ingredients and mix well.

Place large tablespoonfuls of the dough onto the prepared baking tray. Flatten each to a circle of about 6–7 cm, leaving at least 2 cm between each one.

Bake for 12–15 minutes, until the biscuits have risen, spread slightly and turned golden brown. Rotate trays halfway through cooking. Remove from the oven and allow the biscuits to cool slightly before placing them on a wire rack.

These biscuits will keep in an airtight container for up to five days. They also freeze well — thaw at room temperature before eating.

DESSERT

Pavlova is our most famous dessert, a concoction of soft-centred meringue, crisp outside, whipped cream, and fruit topping. This recipe for an All-In-One Pavlova is from Helen Leach's book *The Pavlova Story*, and has been adapted by Mary Browne.

Serves 6–8

PAVLOVA

2 EGG WHITES FROM LARGE EGGS
SEVERAL DAYS OLD, AT ROOM
TEMPERATURE
1½ CUPS CASTER SUGAR
½ TSP VANILLA ESSENCE
1 TSP WHITE VINEGAR
1 TSP CORNFLOUR
4 TBSP BOILING WATER

TOPPING

200 ML CREAM
PEELED AND SLICED KIWIFRUIT,
STRAWBERRIES
OR OTHER FRUIT

Preheat the oven to 180°C with a rack in the centre. Place a piece of non-stick baking paper on an oven tray and draw a 23 cm diameter circle in the centre. Make sure your mixing bowl and beater are thoroughly clean and dry.

Place all the pavlova ingredients in a bowl, adding the boiling water last. Immediately beat the mixture on high speed for 10–12 minutes, until it is shiny and stiff. Spoon into the marked circle and use a spatula to spread evenly.

Bake for 10 minutes, lower the heat to 150°C and then bake a further 45 minutes. Turn off the heat, and allow the pavlova to cool in the oven for at least an hour.

Carefully transfer to a flat serving platter. Whip the cream until stiff and spread on the pavlova. Decorate with fruit.

A BARBECUE

The Kiwi barbecue is a summer tradition — at home, or at the beach or bach. It can be as simple as a few sausages served with a salad, or an elaborate feast of meat, seafood and side dishes. Everything seems to taste better off the barbecue — slightly charred, a little smoky, and all the more delicious for being eaten outdoors. Play your cards right, and there will be fewer dishes to wash afterwards, too. The earliest settlers cooked their meals over an open fire and, as Kiwi chef Al Brown says, 'Give me a knife, a bowl, a chopping board, a set of tongs, a frying pan and some driftwood and I'll cook you dinner.'

A FEED OF WHITEBAIT

These real delicacies are barely big enough to hold in your fingers, and certainly can't be speared with a fork, but one of New Zealand's smallest fish is its biggest delicacy. Whitebait — actually the young of up to five different species of native fish — are harvested and eaten when only 4–5 centimetres long, so you need a fair number of them to get a decent feed. They're caught in nets in the lower reaches of rivers, especially on the west coast of the South Island, and can only be harvested in spring. They are most often eaten in fritters, and the best fritters are almost all egg and whitebait; no flour, thanks. Here's how well-known food writer Lauraine Jacobs makes them.

Makes about 16

2 FRESH ORGANIC EGGS
200 G WHITEBAIT
SEA SALT AND FRESHLY GROUND
BLACK PEPPER
2 TBSP OIL
2 TBSP FRESH BUTTER
LEMON OR LIME WEDGES TO SERVE

Beat the eggs in a bowl until they are light and frothy. Add the whitebait with a generous pinch of salt and plenty of freshly ground black pepper. Mix well.

Take a large, heavy frying pan, and heat the oil and butter together over medium heat. When the butter starts to bubble and spit, add the egg and whitebait mixture in even tablespoonsful (about five or six at a time).

Cook for about 1–2 minutes, then flip each fritter over and cook the other side until golden. Immediately remove to a warmed plate.

Continue cooking in batches of about five fritters until the mixture is finished. Serve at once with fresh lemon or lime wedges.

A NICE GLASS OF PINOT NOIR (OR CHARDONNAY, OR SAUVIGNON BLANC, OR . . .)

For the country the furthest away geographically from the traditional centre of winemaking, we sure make a good drop. Winemaking here was at first a small-scale, domestic operation, with the Marist Brothers of Hawke's Bay turning out the odd extra bottle over and above their communion wine, and didn't really take off until an influx of immigrants from the former Yugoslavia started turning up on our shores in the 1940s and 1950s. Names such as Nobilo, Selak, Delegat and Fistonich (whose label is Villa Maria) were industry pioneers. Those names still appear on labels today, but the biggest growth, in the 1990s, came in the major grape-growing regions of Gisborne, Hawke's Bay and Marlborough, followed by a surge of boutique wineries in Central Otago. There are now more than 700 wineries throughout the country. Far and away our most popular varietal is Sauvignon Blanc (grown mostly in Marlborough), followed by Chardonnay and Pinot Noir, for which Central Otago is becoming justly famous.

DAYS THAT ARE IMPORTANT TO US

ANZAC DAY

The most solemn of public holidays, Anzac Day (25 April) is New Zealand's war memorial day, when we remember the fallen in all the foreign conflicts in which New Zealanders have served. First commemorated in 1916, a year after the disastrous Gallipoli landings in Turkey, it became a full public holiday in 1922. Today it traditionally begins with dawn services throughout the country — and at Gallipoli itself — where crowds of thousands come to pay their respects, before gatherings at Returned and Services' Association (RSA) clubs for servicemen and their families. Since 1922 it's been a tradition on this day to wear a red poppy, a symbol of the First World War battlefields of northern France and Belgium.

WAITANGI DAY

The Treaty of Waitangi, between Māori and the British Crown, was purportedly put forward because Queen Victoria was 'desirous to establish a settled form of Civil Government with a view to avert the evil consequences which must result from the absence of the necessary Laws and Institutions alike to the native population and to Her subjects'. In exchange for 'all the Rights and Privileges of British Subjects', the Māori chiefs of the Confederation of United Tribes were guaranteed 'the full exclusive and undisturbed possession of their Lands and Estates Forests Fisheries and other properties which they may collectively or individually possess so long as it is their wish and desire to retain the same in their possession'.

Did it work out that way? This question is regularly exercised all these years later, in Parliament and through the courts. For this reason Waitangi Day, envisaged in the 1930s as a national day of harmony, can be associated with division and debate. Each year on 6 February, smiling politicians visiting the Treaty Grounds at Waitangi in the Bay of Islands are met by noisy protest from some Māori, while the rest of the country enjoys a bonus summer day off.

MATARIKI

Celebrating the Māori New Year, in the dead of the southern winter, is becoming a new New Zealand tradition. Matariki is timed around the appearance in the southern sky of the constellation known in English as the Pleiades, or the Seven Sisters, which occurs each year in late May or early June, and lasts for a month. The festival has been undergoing a revival since the start of the new millennium, with events being held by museums, marae and community organisations throughout the country. Traditionally it was a time for remembrance of those who had died in the past year, but also an opportunity for feasting and celebrating new beginnings.

HOW WE SAY GOODBYE

Haere rā.
Ka kite anō.
See you.

A SNAPSHOT OF NEW ZEALAND

MĀORI NAME Aotearoa

POPULATION (HUMAN) 4,405,200 (est. 2012)
POPULATION (SHEEP) 31,100,000 (est. 2011)

POPULATION OF THE NORTH ISLAND 3.4 million
POPULATION OF THE SOUTH ISLAND 1 million

CAPITAL CITY Wellington (2011 population
487,700)
LARGEST CITY Auckland (2011 population
1,486,000)

OFFICIAL LANGUAGES English, Māori, New
Zealand Sign Language

AREA 267,707 sq km
AREA UNDER FARMING 145,800 sq km
**AREA PRESERVED IN NATIONAL PARKS, FOREST
RESERVES, ETC.** 80,000 sq km

**% OF POPULATION LIVING WITHIN 10 KM OF
THE COAST** 75 (2006)

PLACE THE FURTHEST FROM THE SEA Cromwell
(119 km from the sea)
NUMBER OF PLEASURE BOATS 350,000 (est.
2006)

DISTANCE FROM BLUFF TO PICTON 922 km and
11 driving hours
DISTANCE FROM WELLINGTON TO CAPE REINGA
1069 km and 13 driving hours

MAIN ETHNIC GROUPS (2006 CENSUS)
New Zealander/New Zealand European
2,810,505
New Zealand Māori 565,329
Asian 354,552 (including Chinese
147,570, Indian 104,583)
Pacific 231,801 (including Samoan
131,103)
British 71,391
Middle Eastern, Latin American and
African 34,743

THE PHOTOGRAPHS

Page 1 Mercury Islands

Page 2 The Tasman River, near Lake Pukaki

Pages 4–5 Kime Hut, Tararua Ranges

Page 6 Blue Pools, Mt Aspiring National Park

Pages 8–9 and cover Cascade Saddle, Mt Aspiring National Park

Pages 10–11 Moke Lake, near Queenstown

Pages 12–13 The waka *Ngā Toki Matawhaoru*, Waitangi, Bay of Islands

Pages 14–15 Meeting house at Wairakei, Central Plateau

Pages 18–19 The Whare Runanga at Waitangi

Pages 22–23 The waka *Maniopoto ki Runga* at Waitangi

Pages 34–35 Half Moon Hut, Molesworth Station, Marlborough

Pages 36–37 The 'Champagne Pool' and sintered terrace, Waiotapu, Rotorua

Pages 40–41, Lake Manapouri

Pages 42–43 All Blacks vs England

Pages 44–45 Blue Lake, Tongariro National Park

Pages 48–49 The Hawkdun Range from the Ida Valley, Central Otago

Pages 50–51 Milford Sound

Pages 52–53 Ninety Mile Beach dunes

Pages 54–55 Tongariro National Park

Pages 56–57 Southern Alps

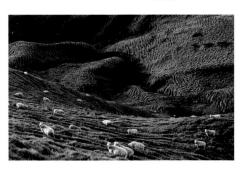

Pages 58–59 Awakino, King Country

Page 61 Winton, Southland

Pages 64–65 Seddon, Marlborough

Pages 66–67 Milking shed, Waikato

Pages 68–69 Geraldine, Canterbury

Pages 71–72 Hawera A&P Show

Pages 102–03 Waipoua Forest, Northland

Page 117 Arrowtown

Pages 118–19 West Matukituki Valley, Mt Aspiring National Park

Pages 120–21 Days Bay, Wellington

Pages 154–55 Te Urewera National Park

Pages 164–65 Arapawa Island, Queen Charlotte Sound

Pages 166–67 Karekare, Waitakere Coast

Pages 168–69 Upper Dunstan Creek and Old Man Peak, Central Otago

Pages 170–71 Clutha River

Pages 172–73 Queenstown

Pages 174–75 Shotover River, Central Otago

Pages 176–77 Luxmore Hut, Central Otago

Page 178 Auckland Harbour Bridge

Pages 180–81 The All Blacks with the Bledisloe Cup

Pages 182–83 Rise Up concert in Hagley Park, Christchurch

Pages 184–85 Wellington vs Central Districts

Pages 188–89 Algies Bay, Mahurangi Peninsula

Pages 190–91 Mimiwhangata, Northland

Pages 194–95 Heliskiing in the Southern Alps, near Wanaka

Pages 196–97 Tongaporutu, Taranaki

Pages 200–01 Tawharanui, north of Auckland

Pages 202–03 Wellington

Pages 220–21 Goat Island Bay, north of Auckland

Pages 222–23 Auckland War Memorial Museum, The Domain, Auckland

Pages 224–25 Paddlers of the waka *Te Ati Awa*, Waitangi Day

Pages 228–29 Abel Tasman National Park

Pages 230–31 Dusky Sound, Fiordland National Park

Pages 232–33 Smails Beach, Otago

Page 239 Cape Palliser, Wairarapa

Page 240 The Catlins coast, Southland

IMAGE & TEXT CREDITS

/Photographs

Aaron McLean 211, 213

Alexander Turnbull Library, Wellington (Kate Sheppard, ref: PUBL-0089-1914-001, 157; Sir Ernest Rutherford, ref: 1/2-050243-F, 158; Jack Lovelock, ref: MSX-2261-118, 159; Bruce McLaren, ref: 1/2-213838-F, 161)

Brian Culy 206

Elizabeth Clarkson 217

Gilbert van Reenen 48–49, 168–69, 170–71

Jae Frew 209

Jane Ussher 163, 219

Jason Hosking 2–3, 6, 40–41, 50–51, 54–55, 56–57, 94–95, 97, 100–01, 108, 112–13, 154–55, 230–31

Patrick Reynolds 12–13, 102–03, 106–07

Photo New Zealand 1 (Kim Christensen), 8–9 (Colin Monteath/Hedgehog House), 10–11 (Miz Matanabe), 14–15 (Rob Tucker), 16–17 (Graeme Mitchell-Anyon), 18–19 (Jeremy Bright), 22–23 (Arno Gasteiger), 30–31 (Angie Harrison), 33 (Paul Kennedy), 42–43 (John Doogan), 52–53 (Mead Norton), 58–59 (Arno Gasteiger), 61 (Arno Gasteiger), 64–65 (Arno Gasteiger), 66–67 (Arno Gasteiger), 68–69 (Arno Gasteiger), 70–71 (Rob Tucker), 104 (Stephen Roke), 114–15 (Paul Mercer), 117 (Chris McLennan), 118–19 (Iain Guillard), 120–21 (Nick Servian), 166–67 (Arno Gasteiger), 172–73 (Graeme Murray), 182–83 (Tony Stewart), 186 (Ann Worthy), 188–89 (Darryl Torckler), 190–91 (Graeme Mitchell-Anyon), 192–93 (Delphine Ducaruge), 194–95 (Larry Prosor), 196–97 (Arno Gasteiger), 199 (Mike Heydon), 200–01 (Arno Gasteiger), 202–03 (Nick Servian), 204–05 (Miles Clarke), 215 (Frank Gasteiger), 220–21 (Darryl Torckler), 222–23 (Kim Christensen), 224–25 (Arno Gasteiger), 232–33 (Simon East), 239 (Jeff Drewitz), 240 (Jason Hosking)

PhotoSport 162

Rob Suisted/Nature's Pic Images 4–5, 34–35, 36–37, 44–45, 93, 98, 110, 164–65, 176–77, 228–229

Rod Morris 90–91

Roger Donaldson Collection 160

Setford News Photo Agency 180–81, 184–85

Shotover Jet 174

Takayuki Yoshida 226–27

Tourism Auckland 178

/Paintings

Cape Maria van Diemen — Waitapu, Stanley Palmer, with permission from the artist 88–89

Cass, Rita Angus, collection Christchurch Art Gallery Te Puna o Waiwhetu; purchased 1955. Reproduced courtesy of the Rita Angus Estate 74–75

Gavin Bishop (*Weaving Earth and Sky*, Random House 2002) 25, 26, 29

Nor'wester in the Cemetery, Willam Sutton, with permission from Christchurch Art Gallery Te Puna o Waiwhetu and Auckland Art Gallery Toi o Tāmaki 76–77

Northland Panels, Colin McCahon, with permission from the McCahon Estate and Museum of New Zealand Te Papa Tongarewa 80–81

Sir Edmund Hillary, Edward Halliday, with permission from Auckland War Memorial Museum 156

Sun shall not burn Thee by day nor moon by night, Don Binney, with permission from Philippa Binney and Auckland Art Gallery Toi o Tāmaki 82–83

Taranaki, Christopher Perkins, with permission from Rachel Wren and Auckland Art Gallery Toi o Tāmaki 78–79

Tarawera Rest Stop, Dick Frizzell, with permission from the artist 86–87

Timeless Land, Grahame Sydney, with permission from the artist 72–73, 84–85

/Text

Anzac biscuits recipe, Dean Brettschneider (*Global Baker*, Random House 2007) 210

'At the Bay', Katherine Mansfield (*Katherine Mansfield Short Stories*, Vintage 2008) 123–53

Cheesy scones recipe, Jo Seagar (*It's Easier than You Think*, Random House 2010) 208

'Elegy in the Clutha Valley', Brian Turner (*Elemental*, Godwit 2012) 170–71

Gingerbread recipe, Alexander Tylee (*Pipi*, Random House 2012) 207

'Landfall in Unknown Seas', Allen Curnow, with permission from the Curnow Estate 166–67

Māori words in common usage, from '100 Māori words everyone should know', and 'A Māori word a day', www.nzistory.net.nz 20–21

Pavlova recipe, Mary Browne (*A Treasury of New Zealand Baking*, edited by Lauraine Jacobs, Random House 2009) 212

'The Creation Myth', Robert Sullivan (*Weaving Earth and Sky*, Random House 2002) 24–29

'The Skeleton of the Moa in the Canterbury Museum, Christchurch', Allen Curnow, with permission from the Curnow Estate 168–69

Whitebait fritters recipe, Lauraine Jacobs (*Everlasting Feast*, Random House 2013) 216

A RANDOM HOUSE BOOK published by Random House New Zealand
18 Poland Road, Glenfield, Auckland, New Zealand

For more information about our titles go to www.randomhouse.co.nz

A catalogue record for this book is available from the
National Library of New Zealand

Random House New Zealand is part of the Random House Group
New York   London   Sydney   Auckland   Delhi   Johannesburg

First published 2013

ISBN 978 1 77553 441 9

Design: Carla Sy
Cover photograph: Photo New Zealand (Colin Monteath/Hedgehog House)

Printed in China by Everbest Printing Co Ltd